In Search of
Safe Brave Spaces

WITHDRAWN FROM
T N L.S.

MW00982287

In Search of Safe Brave Spaces

K. Greg Smith

Rock's Mills Press
Oakville, Ontario
2021

Thompson Nicola Regional Library
300 - 465 VICTORIA STREET
KAMLOOPS, BC V2C 2A9

Published by
Rock's Mills Press
www.rocksmillspress.com

Copyright © 2021 by K. Greg Smith.
All rights reserved. This book or any portion thereof may not be reproduced or used in any manner whatsoever without the express written permission of the publisher except for the use of brief quotations in a book review.

Cover design: Woopzoop Studio

For information about this book, including bulk, bookstore, and library orders, email us at customer.service@rocksmillspress.com.

3 5444 00478540 7

Dedication

This book is dedicated to my life partner Josette
whose love and encouragement regularly keep me
both safe and brave.

Also, to my parents Kenn and Ruth
who provided me the space to discover and be my unique self.

And in memory of my brother-in-law Kent
whose giving heart and acts of service continue to inspire me.

Contents

Acknowledgements

Throughout my life I have been blessed with many friends and family members who have contributed to my safe brave journey so far. Thank you to the following people:

- Josette: For always believing in me, encouraging me, challenging me and loving me;
- Danica: For your courage and wisdom to help me see beyond my truth to a broader truth;
- Jenssen and Michelle (Woopzoop Studio): For your creativity, patience and passion to help bring the idea of safe brave spaces to life visually;
- Mom and Dad: For being my "life living" example and champion of me "being ME";
- Mike Farley: For your safe brave coaching/friendship, supporting me through the activation of safe brave spaces—the book, the circles and the movement;
- Karen and Ian: For sparking my confidence, nudging me to action and being first to champion;
- My family cheerleaders: Bob, Sylvia, Jeff, Karen, Norma, Beth, Sean, Kat, Jess, Rob, Evan, Zack, Brodie, Ola and Bisi, for your encouragement and support;
- Friends, early readers & promoters: Allister, Casey, Christi S, Fiona, Jan O, Phil Donne, Phil Drouillard, Robert A, Sheena W, Steve G, Shelley, Marlene and Wayne;

- My Lighthouse NINE Group partners Phil, Marnie, Drew, Dave, Cindy, Christi, Gemma, Kim, Nancy, Corinne, Sheena for listening, championing and supporting;
- Sarah McVanel-Viney and my fellow authors in the GreatnessBizBook Writing Intensive who held me accountable and helped release my confidence and commitment to writing;
- My publisher, David Stover, of Rock's Mills Press, who shepherded me through the new and exciting world of book publishing.

In Search of
Safe Brave Spaces

1. Introduction

As a coach, one exercise that I often recommend for clients—and that has been helpful for me—is what's called a "Meaningful Experiences Journal." This simple process of reflecting and capturing moments of both fulfillment and challenge in our lives widens perspective and allows us to more clearly see repeatable patterns and themes. Personally, at least every five years, and always within times of flux, I refresh my journal and inevitably discover evolving insights.

A few years ago, I found myself in a tough season of my life, both personally and professionally. Returning to this powerful reflection exercise, I discovered a new insight which for me brought a clear focus, renewed energy, and a sense of peace and hope. The insight was the gift of *safe brave spaces*, and it sparked a desire to discover and capture situations, people and resources that had resulted in important changes and moments of realization in my life. I was able to more fully achieve my individual potential and help to enable potential in others.

The result is this book.

As I shared early drafts with friends and family, I became aware of stories of other individuals, teams and communities who had discovered similar themes and had begun their own journeys. One dialogue led to another, and suddenly a sense of momentum and possibility emerged.

I have been blessed and recognize that, as a white, cisgender older man raised in a relatively healthy, stable middle-class home, I have many privileges. Within that context I have also always been seen as

1

different, well-liked but never fully fitting in, more emotional than most men (my sister claims that I am half-woman, which I consider a blessing), and possessing a deep sense there is more to me and to this world, and that there is a better way of being.

My journey has never been one with a clear plan, and yet my head is always full of possibilities and curiosity about what is happening and what could happen. Many of my friends knew what they were going to do at a very young age, while I have mostly moved towards where I was drawn, being pulled towards things and people that interested me or where I sensed that I could make a difference. Recently I discovered through a tool called the enneagram that I am an "enthusiastic visionary," which is described as a quick-thinking, experience-seeking, optimistic, passionate, pain-avoiding, future-driven individual with strong "considerate helper" and "peacemaker" gifts. This is not my first such assessment—throughout my career in operations and human resources I have completed and am now certified in many assessments and tools; however, this report resonated strongly with me as indicating a deep truth about who I am and how I am. What I most appreciate about this instrument is that it simply describes one's innate gifts, which are first awakened in response to one's own fears: how those gifts can show up (both positively and negatively) and how you can begin accessing your fuller self, which may have been left untouched or underdeveloped because of over-dependency on your core type. This idea that we have innate gifts that help us survive and, in many cases, succeed really resonated with me as being true. Equally exciting was the opportunity to understand and access untapped abilities to release even greater impact and potential.

Over the course of my life and later in my career, I innately understood that the most fulfilling relationships, communities and organizations that I experienced were those that provided the safe space to be my "full self" and to continue to explore and release both my heart and my mind. They were also environments that were built on the belief that everything happened "in-between" and the best way to speed up both personal and collective potential was through communities that enabled, supported and protected caring, curious and courageous spaces. When I found myself with the opportunity to help create these spaces, I began to see a better way of being and the prospect of a more fulfilling, more productive, more connected life.

My first hope with this book is to share with you some things I have discovered over the past 50 years from amazing individuals who themselves shared pieces of wisdom that have helped me assemble a clearer understanding of my life puzzle and what I believe can be a framework for others as they continue on their individual journeys. Some of these people wrote books that have inspired me, challenged me, frustrated me and activated me. I have included my favourite models and ideas from these incredible people within this book and created some new ones of my own. Other people are what I think of as "footnotes" in either my life or the lives of those who have influenced me. I love this idea of being a "footnote." I think it is something that I have always strived to be. I think of a "footnote" as someone who influences, teaches, cares and supports by being who they are and doing what they do. If you investigate all the great minds and world shifters throughout history, you will discover the "footnotes" in their lives—those individuals who showed up exactly when needed, who presented an idea, some support or some wisdom that opened up a new door for others in their journey.

The second goal of this book is to share some things I have tried and what I have learned along the way. The stories you hear will include moments of full joy when I found myself in what some may call "flow"; when I felt both a witness and participant in something bigger than myself, connected with others im moving towards a grander truth. Other stories will capture the crashes in my life, times when I extended myself too far, felt out of control and without purpose or balance.

When I was a young boy my "Nana Smith" shared an early piece of wisdom that at the time I didn't quite understand but today, as I come closer to her age, I now know to be true. "Greg," she said, "throughout your life you will have highs and you will have lows. During the highs you will feel that these are the 'best times' and through your lows you will feel that these are the 'worst times.' It is only upon reflection, five or ten years out, that you will discover that neither of these alternatives is true. You will see that the worst was best and the best was worst. The key is what you take away and learn from each moment."

I have often discovered that what I thought were the best times were in retrospect periods when I was too me-focused and therefore missed some important opportunities and relational connections. What I thought were the worst times I now realize were times of significant growth, when I chose to learn and allow myself to be supported within the community. Hindsight is informative and, if we pause and reflect, informs us about where we are and highlights pathways forward. The key is that we learn and continue with our journey, as Simba learned from his guide, Rafiki, in the animated film *The Lion King*. After Rafiki hits Simba with his walking stick, Simba cries out, "What's that for?"

"It doesn't matter, it is in the past," Rafiki replies, and then swings his stick at Simba again, who this time quickly moves to avoid being struck. Although the first incident was indeed "in the past," it provided a key learning moment and an important insight around how to move forward.

Before, however, you embark on a journey, you need to determine what it is you are seeking. For me, what I sought was something I would soon describe as "safe brave spaces."

Safe Brave Spaces

In June 2016, my life unraveled. In the course of only a year, painful and confusing experiences disrupted my life. It all began the previous summer, first with my uncle collapsing in my arms and, soon after, passing away, followed by watching my best friend since childhood wither away with brain cancer and my spouse contract a virus that left her in and out of hospital and despondent. Throughout this period, I was working with a boss whose values were the polar opposite of mine and who didn't value my contribution. By the time I was informed that I "no longer fit" into the organization, I had lost all confidence, personal value and desire to impact. This was the most troubling period of my life, which up to that point had been successful and meaningful.

Although I "left well" and my personality and my words projected an attitude of "I am good, this is good, I am excited about the new chapter of my life," internally behind this glossy self-created personal brand I felt like a plane that had lost both engines and was being piloted by someone who had never flown before. For the first time in decades I was out of work, felt totally out of control, not valued, with no clear view of where I should go and what I should do. My misplaced belief that I needed to keep positive while my wife struggled with depression and anxiety, driven by the declarations from many doctors that her painful, unresolvable illness would continue the rest of her life, only exacerbated the façade I was maintaining. As I mentioned earlier, I am a thinker, and therefore the first place I went in this crisis was somewhere that I trusted and which had brought me success for much of my life: my mind. Here, I thought, was the best place to find a way out of my circumstances. This unfortunately resolved nothing and in fact sped up my downward spiral as I realized that depending on myself and my mind alone was not enough. It was at this moment, when I had lost all sense of control in almost every area of my life simultaneously, that I captured my perspective around the importance of safe brave spaces.

Within this place of brokenness, I finally let go and opened up. I'm not sure if it was a choice or a collapse, but I know that at some moment within this spiral I realized that I had to let go of my grip and allow others to hold me up. When I did that, my façade fell away, and I entered a place that some call "flow." I felt both a witness and participant in something bigger than myself, connected with others in moving towards a grander purpose and truth. In this state of "flow" I felt safe, peaceful and present, with a glimmer of hope that things would be okay preparing me for a brave new day. I also recognized that this was a familiar place, one that I had previously visited before in times of extreme joy and deep sorrow. I think it is amazing how complex human consciousness is and how in tapping into our fuller selves we access a deeper wisdom collected over our entire lifetime.

Following my release of control, these memories of what I now describe as safe brave spaces tumbled out of my mind. They included a near-death experience at age sixteen, the day of my marriage, the birth of my children, and a severe health emergency during a mission trip in the Dominican Republic. All of these events were deeply meaningful experiences that began with spikes in energy and disruption, included a strong sense of love and gratitude, and created a unique space of pause and presence to something bigger in the moment. As I reflected on these experiences, I pondered what contributed to these safe brave spaces, what was enabled because of them, and what I might do to create these spaces more frequently within myself, in my one-on-one relationships and in my broader communities. Thus began my search for safe brave paces.

Before I investigated how to contribute to and create safe brave spaces I wanted to more clearly understand what had been enabled within myself because of them. As prior work in the study of "flow" focuses on this concept of tapping into our full self, I began reviewing my initial list of meaningful experiences through the lenses of the three parts of the self: thinking, feeling and doing. From a thinking perspective, when in those moments, I was caring, confident, curious and courageous. From a feeling perspective, when I was in this "flow" state I experienced peace, joy, gratitude and freedom. The resulting actions, the doing, were focused, impactful and purposeful.

Viewing matters through these three lenses, I saw that safe brave space is not a thing or a destination, but a state of being and relating. It isn't something that you achieve, but something that you continually create. As you activate it within yourself, you realize an ever-expanding level of potential. Through this emerging potential you experience greater joy, peace and freedom. I define joy as a source of delight and well-being. It is when my heart is filled with gratefulness in the moment, where my heart is fully engaged, and I feel connected to something bigger than myself. Joy and peace are intertwined as one enhances the other. Peace is a place of "pause" where one feels fully equipped and prepared for this moment. In moments of peace we experience a stillness in our body, mind and heart where we become a joyous witness. Joy and peace lead to freedom. Freedom to choose, to act, to live more fully. These are the moments in our lives when we experience a resistance-free flow, letting go and fully showing up to the experience and to those we are experiencing it with.

When we experience this emerging potential, we recognize that it is not something new but something hidden within us. Through personal reflection, I have discovered past moments where I have found myself in this place before. It was, however, in this recent troubled time that I more fully realized the opportunity and worked to discover methods to activate it more often.

The beauty of safe brave spaces is that anyone can activate them within themselves. It simply requires us to commit to, and focus on, the strengthening of two elements: *safe*, by which I mean understanding, accepting and trusting yourself and others; and *brave*—doing, acting, releasing the unencumbered freedom to stand for what you believe in and supporting others to do the same. *Safe* and *brave* are complementary to each other; as I work on one, the other strengthens. As I committed to developing my personal safe brave space I—

- Felt free to **be** me and to **bring** my "whole self" to each situation;
- Gained **confidence** and trust in who I am and what I bring;
- Became more **curious** about and came to better value the unique contribution of others; and
- More **courageously** expressed my insights, ideas and perspectives, while letting go of bias and remaining open to others.

With this definition I began to do some research into current thinking around the topic and quickly discovered some amazing work in the areas of creating psychologically safe environments and a relatively new surge of books, ideas and research around enhancing and activating the ability for individuals and communities to be brave. Two leading thinkers in these areas include Amy Edmondson, whose book *The Fearless Organization* laid the foundation for the safe workplace movement, and Brené Brown, whose remarkable work includes her most recent books *Daring Greatly* and *Dare to Lead*. All of this work really resonated with me and was an important contributor to the release of "flow." As I reviewed the research and application of these separate movements, I have also come to believe that it is the interdependency of feeling and being both safe and brave that is the key. For each of us to contribute and take part at our highest levels we need to grow both these capacities. As we grow one, it impacts and refines the other.

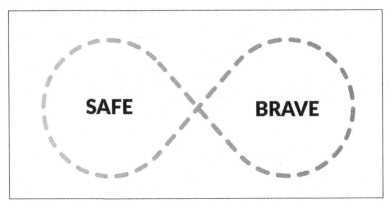

As Maya Angelou once said, "Without courage we cannot practice any other virtue with consistency. We can't be kind, true, merciful, generous, or honest." As I reflected on my own life, I could see times where I had more fully lived the behaviours that contributed to safe brave spaces. Throughout my career and in my personal life, others have acknowledged that one of my innate gifts is to quickly create an open space in which others feel comfortable to trust and share. This ability to create "safe space" has been a contributor to my personal growth and the development of the teams, communities and organizations within which I have worked. As I reflected on this expanding insight of the interdependency of safe and brave spaces, I recognized that in order to more fully release and express my potential and that of those whom I support, I needed to strengthen my ability to be brave. Most of us have either a more evolved "brave muscle" or "safe muscle," and many of us have endured circumstances that resulted in one or both muscles becoming weakened. The glorious thing is that, like our physical muscles, we can build habits and access tools and equipment to rebuild and enhance both our safe and brave muscles to enable safe brave spaces for ourselves and those around us.

Also, much like a physical workout, to achieve our goals we need a plan, and the journey is more likely to succeed if you engage others in your plan. As when we decide to start exercising again, recognizing the need to work on our safe and brave muscles often occurs when we reach a place of no other choices. In my personal experience, the times of greatest growth occur during moments of greatest suffering, and each time I found myself there, my recovery started with the encouragement and support of a good friend. I hope that some of the ideas and the stories shared within this book will help you both discover and strengthen your personal safe and brave muscles and enable you to help create safe brave spaces within the communities you touch.

One additional insight that emerged from my expanded research and investigation into my meaningful experiences was the correlation between work and volunteer experience and organizational cultures. In each of my most positive experiences, the organizations promoted and supported programs and environments that enabled safe brave spaces. Beyond these personal experiences I knew of other companies who believed in this approach, many of which are discussed in one of my favourite business books, *Firms of Endearment*, by Raj Sisodia, Jag Sheth and David B. Wolfe. It would seem that companies such as Whole Foods, Costco, Southwest Airlines, Patagonia, IKEA and SAS continue to thrive compared to their competitors due in part to creating environments that connect all of their stakeholders at a much deeper level, creating the foundation for activating whole selves. These organizations lived what I had recognized as the key behaviours within safe-brave communities:

- A commitment to discovering, enabling and valuing individual uniqueness;
- A culture and supporting frameworks to release individual and collective gifts and voices;
- A courageous community that respectfully challenges members to refine great ideas; and
- An alignment of strategy, structure, system/processes/policies, rewards and people to enable safe/brave spaces.

Inspired by these initial insights, I formally began my search for safe brave spaces. I quickly recognized that the journey towards them involved five key stages:

1. Preparing for the journey
2. Starts within ME
3. Accelerates between "YOU & ME"
4. Flourishes through "WE"
5. Begins wherever you are

In this book, I will dive deeper into each of these five components. In each section I provide ideas, insights and tools that I found helpful for me on my journey and some examples of situations where I have attempted to apply them. I have used each of these tools during my journey and although I may not continue to use all of them today, they were helpful at the time and I often refer back to them when necessary.

Early in my exploration I recognized the value of having a map, a journal and a travel pack with tools to assist in the journey. As a kid, one thing I loved about family vacations was going to the automobile club to get a "TripTik." Those over forty may recall this was a collection of mini-maps with the road map printed on one side of the sheet and important attractions and other information on the other. As you came to the end of one mini-map, you flipped it over to see the next leg of your journey. Each of the kids in our family took turns being the navigator and in an age with no built-in DVD players, iPads or cell phones it was one of the most exciting experiences during a road trip. What made the TripTik special was that it was easy to handle, straightforward to read and logically assembled so that one step led to another.

Aside from the TripTik, on our family trips we also brought along the automobile association's detailed guidebooks covering each state or province that we were visiting. You might think of the book you're now holding as the equivalent of those guidebooks. Early readers of the manuscript told me they found it interesting, personal and "meaty," and that they had never come across a book that pulled together so many helpful insights and tools, allowing them to pick what worked best for them. And just as the "TripTik," an easily accessible tool helping you understand where you were at any given moment, complemented the bigger guidebook, I have created a companion tool to this book—*My SBS Learning Journal*— to serve as your "TripTik" as you work towards understanding and discovering safe brave spaces within yourself, in your relationships and in the communities you serve and support.

In each chapter of the book you will find insights, tools and questions coupled with stories that help provide context and application. As on those family road trips of yesteryear, to fully experience the trip it is important to get out of the car to try some new things. To facilitate these "side trips" you will see throughout the book a "pause" icon. At these "pause points" I have provided questions to help you reflect upon what you've read, identify what resonates most, and select ideas and tools to experiment with as you begin your journey. These pauses are not mandatory; however, I recommend them as the best way to prioritize what resonates most with you and what instinctively you want to try at each stage of the journey.

As mentioned, throughout the book I will also provide additional references and resources that I have found helpful. These will be important to those "family members" who love to research destinations and insist on stopping at each tourist attraction during the trip. Although this can sometimes frustrate those who want to get to their destination quickly, there are often amazing discoveries and surprises that we uncover when we take the time to stop along the way and dig deeper. All these forms, tools and articles can be found at **www.safebravespaces.com.**

I was writing this book when the Covid-19 crisis hit. Throughout the crisis, amongst the tremendous pain and uncertainty, there has been a spike in love, care and connection within diverse communities, driven by a shared experience and a commitment to other-centredness. The power of this intention and the impact it is having are among the most beautiful things that I have experienced so far in my life, and give me great hope in our future. Across the world we have witnessed individuals and communities creating and contributing to safe brave spaces for themselves. A further shift happened following the horrific death of George Floyd in police custody in Minneapolis in May 2020, an event which has resulted in many of us reflecting on the gaps and inconsistencies around the provision of safe brave spaces for all. The outpouring of support driving peaceful demonstrations for important changes to existing systems and behaviours has challenged me personally to do more and further enhanced my faith in our collective ability to advance this journey towards safe brave spaces.

The success of this journey will only happen through a commitment within and across communities. Genuine change needs to start within ME, accelerates between YOU & ME, and flourishes through WE. Throughout my life I have seen the power of positive momentum and I am sensing a lot of that in our world today. Momentum is enhanced through stories and through the open sharing of our experiences and the resources that have enabled our success (including the mistakes that have informed deeper awareness). To support this positive momentum, we have created a couple of portals to provide a platform to capture and share what you are experiencing, what you've tried, what you've discovered, and to create a place of healthy dialogue to learn and grow together. We hope that sharing and reading these stories and ideas will further enhance that momentum and that as you tap into the resulting energy and love, you will sense a full release of your potential and the potential of those around you as you create safe brave spaces. If you are interested in joining this movement in search of safe brave spaces, check out and contribute at either www.safebravespaces.com or on our YouTube channel, "Safe Brave Spaces."

Welcome to the first "pause point." Reflect and consider the things you have just read in the introduction, and take a few minutes to capture "your story so far." The questions below can also be found in *My SBS Learning Journal.*

- What are the key events and experiences that have most shaped that journey to date?
- Who are the people who have influenced you most? How have they influenced you?
- What is your current state of safe and brave?
- What is your desired state of safe and brave?

2. Safe Brave Spaces: Preparing for the Journey

Any seasoned traveller will tell you that the key to a successful adventure is to ensure you are well-planned and well-resourced prior to starting out. The first section helped prepare you by providing a definition of safe brave spaces and laying out a pathway towards discovery. This second section will introduce you to some key tools to better equip and support you on the journey. These include the importance of energy, the power of pause, and the opportunity to ELOPE.

The Importance of Energy

"A human being is a deciding being. Between stimulus and response there is a space. In that space is our power to choose our response. In our response lies our growth and our freedom."
—Viktor Frankl

When I was in my early twenties, while applying for a new job with Toys "R" Us, I discovered the insight that "everything is energy." The opportunity was my first significant leap in HR and the role was to lead learning and development for the Canadian organization. The memory of this moment is so clear that I know it was an "a-ha" moment that was important for me to understand and learn from. As I shared in the introduction, these discoveries rarely come to light until later in life, and that was true for this situation. I remember arriving for this stage of the selection process, which was a live presentation on a topic of my choosing attended by the Canadian president, the CFO, and the VP of marketing. I was well prepared and had what I felt was a very visual, practical and impactful presentation on adult learning featuring a unique perspective on how to engage others. I remember sitting in the lobby on a bench covered in black leather tucked away under the stairwell that would lead me to the executive boardroom on the second floor. Across from me was the receptionist, who was pleasant and very busy, and the rest of the room was empty. I was alone and at first slowly, then more quickly began an in-depth conversation with myself about my lack of ability and preparedness for this event. Normally I am an outgoing, positive and confident individual. I love connecting with people and sharing interesting and creative ideas to make life better. However, sitting alone with myself, the internal demons of self-doubt spread "fake news" throughout my very being until I began sweating, breathing shallowly and spinning out of control. Within ten minutes I had gone from high confidence to high anxiety, focus to spin, hope to despair.

Most of us have at one time or another found ourselves so full of worries, concerns, ideas, and biases, preoccupied with the past or the future, that it is hard to hear or sense anything else. I am a "head person," a thinker who seeks ideas and loves to explore pathways in my head. This is a gift that allows me to see patterns and strategies more quickly than many people; however, it also can cause me to get lost in spin, both positive and negative, leading me to miss the bigger and deeper insight. That morning I was in a negative spin.

Fortunately, amid this spin, something disrupted my "mind storm." I can't remember what it was. Did the receptionist ask me if I wanted some water, or did someone enter the room? Maybe I said a prayer, maybe a door slammed. Something broke the spin and allowed me to pause. It was as if my total being was in the midst of a hurricane and, somehow, I found myself in the eye where there is peace and calm and a clear sense of focus. Within this safe space the following simple insight came into very sharp focus: "Everything is energy and we simply need to learn how to channel it."

Within seconds of seeing this "truth" my body relaxed. The clarity and simplicity of this idea resonated so fully with me I could sense a shift. My body was still electrified; however, I had a sense of control over that energy. I somehow knew that I had the power to choose what to do with this surge of energy that I was feeling. This clarity allowed me to pause and regain what was true in this moment, that—

- I was prepared;
- I had a great idea (shared by someone I valued and knew was an expert in the area);
- I believed in the idea and it aligned with my yet-to-be formally defined purpose of "creating spaces that released individual and collective potential"; and
- I knew this was something that during previous interviews I had discovered that the organization needed.

With these facts reconfirmed, I imagined hitting a switch to redirect the energy from anxiety to resourcing my hope for the situation. I envisioned what it would look and feel like as they heard my message, grew from the knowledge, and got excited by the possibilities. I saw myself leaving the meeting fired up, excited and fulfilled. As I was lost in this dream, I heard the words, "Mr. Smith, you can go up now…."

Although I can be a bit of a dreamer, I had experienced nothing like this before. With this one simple insight around energy, I was recharged and more focused than I had ever been. This new discovery unveiled to me the fact that when I let go of the spin and anxiety, I could see more clearly. I felt totally in "flow" and delivered the presentation with poise, confidence and clarity. The energy in the room was high and positive, and the dialogue that followed was full of engagement. I knew that I had hit a home run, evidenced by an offer by the end of the day.

After my interview I went home and shared this odd experience with my wife and a few friends. However, as is true for most of us, I got distracted, chalked it up as just another positive experience and buried it away in my memory. The company offered me the job, which I decided after much reflection not to take, and the big idea settled down deep in my psyche.

Fast forward 15 years. I am coaching my twenty-year-old daughter as she works through a stressful situation when the deep-buried memory and learning of that day bubbles up. I shared my story with her and asked if she would like to try an experiment making use of this insight. She agreed and together we walked through the following six steps to ACCEPT:

- **Acknowledge** that what you are feeling is simply energy that you can channel.
- **Capture** the energy to channel it to something more positive (imagine you have the power to do so).
- **Confirm** the real "truths" of the situation—what you know is really, really true (thank you, Byron Katie).
- **Envision** the situation or outcomes that you desire, for yourself and for others.
- **Pivot** your energy towards achieving those desired outcomes.
- **Transform** the outcomes.

Now my daughter is a bit of a sci-fi geek, so the idea of energy shifts immediately appealed to her. However, as we walked through the steps, I could visibly see a shift overtake her. It was as if she was strengthening right in front of me. You could see a wave of peace followed by control and confidence flow over her. I could still sense the energy, but there was a different vibe and vibration. While she answered my questions, I captured her key insights and then together we built a plan. Within 30 minutes, my daughter experienced the same transformation that I had experienced 15 years ago. This shared experience awakened the original insight around energy that I thought had been buried but in fact had been bubbling within me ever since that interview.

I began reflecting on other experiences where energy played a role in my life. Earlier I mentioned that I tend to be less of a planner, instead moving towards areas of interest. I soon discovered that since that original incident I had unconsciously been drawn back to this idea of the importance of energy in the books I read, the assessments I took and the people I met. Each time I encountered the topic, it resonated within me as something I sensed was true. The two most important "power boosts" of learning and awareness around this idea of energy were through an assessment tool, the Kolbe Index, and through insights and a plan based upon the book *The Power of Full Engagement* by Jim Loehr and Tony Schwartz.

The Kolbe Index

Not long after the Toys "R" Us experience I took my first assessment, the Kolbe A™ Index. This tool has since become one of the first things I introduce folks to at the beginning of their self-discovery journeys. It is a simple-to-use tool that helps individuals and teams to discover their unique way of problem-solving and decision-making, ways which maximize the efficient use of their innate energy. My report describes my "modus operandi (MO)" as a "5384 Quick Start," terminology which means I am a forward-thinking individual who loves change and brainstorming. My other modes reveal a person who likes some facts (not too many!) and prefers not to get locked into too much process and structure. When I am striving to achieve something and find myself in environments that align to my "MO," I more effectively leverage my energy and things just seem smoother and easier. I suspect that I had had previous experiences when I was in "flow" and more efficiently leveraging my energy, but the combination of this experience and the insights from this tool propelled me to want to uncover more information about energy. (The Kolbe A™ Index is a trademark of Kathy Kolbe and Kolbe Corp. All rights reserved. It is used here with permission. For more information visit www.kolbe.com.)

The Power of Full Engagement

Two years later a friend gave me a copy of *The Power of Full Engagement: Managing Energy Not Time* by Jim Loehr and Tony Schwartz, and I broadened and deepened my understanding about the importance of energy and its impact on our lives. The timing of the gift of this book was perfect as I was just beginning two weeks of vacation at a cottage surrounded by magnificent trees and close to a private, isolated beach. Nestled in this idyllic environment, I was immediately captured by the first sentence of the book where the authors stated: "We live in digital time. Our rhythms are rushed, rapid fire and relentless, our days carved up into bits and bytes. We celebrate breadth rather than depth, quick reaction more than considered reflection. We skim across the surface, alighting for brief moments at dozens of destinations but rarely remain for long at any one. We race through our lives without pausing to consider who we really want to be or where we really want to go. We're wired up, but we're melting down."

As I read those first few words an internal bell rang as I observed the truth of that statement both for myself and for those around me. Over the next week my initial instincts around energy were reinforced and my depth of understanding of powerful insights and practical exercises to access and manage my energy was further enhanced. In their research and work, Loehr and Schwartz concluded that our individual and collective capacity is a function of our ability to expend and recover energy, and that every thought, feeling and action has an energy consequence. Having trained many of the world's most renowned athletes, they also recognized that optimal energy, engagement and performance required drawing on four separate but related sources of energy: physical, emotional, mental and spiritual capacity. These ideas really resonated with me. Throughout my life I had always strived to keep physically healthy by working out, mentally healthy by reading and learning, emotionally healthy by building good relationships, and spiritually healthy by participating in my faith community. What was new to me was the authors' insight around the connection to energy and how the four energy sources connected to each other.

The book led me through a practical process that helped me complete a "health check" of each quadrant and identify simple steps to uncover and manage each energy source. As I reflected on my current total energy map and also on the last few years, I recognized three important things: (1) There is a dynamic relationship between the four quadrants and one dimension affects the others. (2) I had a history of swinging my focus from one quadrant to another, normally driven by guilt or pain. (3) By understanding and leveraging the natural flow between the quadrants, I more consistently released my fullest energy, engagement and performance. I incorporated this last idea, the power of integration, into a personal growth plan, which became an important accelerator of my whole self, and now in hindsight I see contributed towards strengthening my personal safe and brave muscles. I entitled this personal growth plan my "ME maximizer plan" and filtered all of my goals through four questions:

- How does this goal strengthen and release my physical energy? (Body and Health Focus)
- How does this goal strengthen and release my emotional energy? (Feelings and Relational Focus)
- How does this goal strengthen and release my mental energy? (Thinking and Learning Focus)
- How does this goal strengthen and release my spiritual energy? (Higher Purpose Focus)

The goals that made it on my list had to combine at least two of those filters and often covered three. Examples that I continue today are listening to audiobooks or podcasts while on the elliptical trainer, often taking notes on my cellphone (mental and physical), and taking regularly scheduled walks with my family in our local park, creating a space for connectivity and conversation while enjoying the beauty of nature (emotional and spiritual). Later in the book you will see areas where I have incorporated this thinking into my evolved personal frameworks; however, it remains one of the most important foundational pieces in my journey towards safe brave spaces.

Discovering this deeper awareness of energy and finding better ways to understand it and manage it, I also wanted to find ways to better recognize when the "storms" were coming and how to prepare for and minimize the negative impact.

What is interesting about storms is that they result from a collision of energy. These energy disruptions normally come about because of an interaction and/or experience with another person and usually show up physically first with a sensation in my body. The challenge for me was that I wasn't great at picking up on these signals early enough to prevent the storm. To better understand my storms, I needed to map my energy and my responses to the energy of others. Over two weeks, leveraging what I call my Energy Exploration Exercise (EEE), I tracked every time I sensed my energy spike and captured my answers to the following questions (I used the Day One app on my phone, but you could just as easily use a notepad):

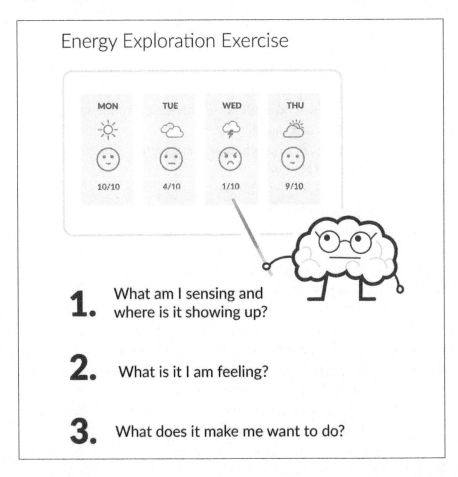

Reviewing my answers helped me to discern certain patterns that helped me better sense the energy and predict and prepare for the storm. It was as though I had discovered my internal Doppler radar. It didn't stop the storms from coming, but it positioned me to better adapt and respond more quickly and effectively to them.

Understanding the impact of energy and my personal mind storms is a work in progress. I am making some progress, and yet there are still times when I recognize that I have missed the warnings and the damage has already been done. As with any habit, awareness is the first step and helps me see the surges coming, something which proved important while working in quarantine with my family during the Covid-19 pandemic. The more people there are together in close quarters, the more likely that energy collisions and storms will occur. Strengthening my early warning signals and better understanding the impact of the disruption on me was an important first step. The second step, one that was equally important, was to strengthen my ability to pause when I felt a storm approaching.

Take some time to reflect on the things you have just read around accessing energy and consider the following:

- What resonated most as "true" for you within this section? Why? What most challenges and/or churns within you? Why?
- How aware are you of your energy shifts and spikes (high/medium/low)?
- Over the next two weeks track your personal energy using the EEE (see **www.safebravespaces.com**). Note what patterns and themes are emerging and how accurate your level of awareness is.

The Power of Pause

Making choices to channel my energy requires me to discover and strengthen my personal ability to pause. As Anne Lamott has suggested, "Almost everything will work again if you unplug it for a few minutes, including you." Sometimes we simply have to unplug or have someone—or something—unplug us. In our current world, at least up until the Covid-19 crisis, I found myself often overloaded and distracted, both with the world that I had created and the one that was being forced upon me at every moment. It is curious for me that this book, which has been in my brain for at least 15 years, is only now being realized through a forced environment of "pause" created by a state of emergency and a requirement to self-isolate. The reality is that, no matter how challenging our current state is, we will eventually return to a "new normal" world where the high volume of pressures, ideas and opinions will again cloud and disrupt the ability to pause. (Some of you, of course, have never left that environment and, if anything, are actually experiencing an even higher level of pressure within the current crisis.) I hope that out of the shifts and pain we will discover deeper awareness of ourselves and others to help create a better new normal. For me personally, this current situation has definitely accelerated my shift, my growth, and deepened the discovery and appreciation of the power of pause.

Pausing is difficult for someone who likes to keep busy and gets their value from accomplishing things, connecting with and serving others. My definition of success has been largely driven by "doing" and in the process I had unfortunately lost the art of "being." When your mechanism for delivering the "doing" disappears, it leaves you with a huge vacuum that is difficult to fill. Sitting still is not one of my strong points and fortunately I found a short-term alternative to filling the "doing bucket" by more fully activating two of my favourite activities: exploring new ideas and connecting with others. The positive aspect of this initial response was that it temporarily got me out of my head and into community. It filled my natural desire to engage and learn; however, without understanding and accessing my heart, I frantically jumped back and forth between the thinking and the doing, in the process speeding up the mind storms that I described earlier. As I began more consistently to be aware of the energy boosts, I found myself more frequently arriving at the requirement to pause. I knew that I needed to learn how to "be" and to "see" in this state of pause. Fortunately, I had begun some helpful practices over the last several years that provided me momentum in this area. Interestingly enough, the discovery and development of these practices also began during a period of high-energy spikes created by tremendous stress, loss and suffering and were sparked by a reluctant acceptance of a gift.

Mindfulness, Meditation and the Gift of the Swing
"Mindfulness gives you time. Time gives you choices. Choices skillfully made lead to freedom."
—Bhante Henepola Gunaratana

I consider myself a spiritual person and my tradition teaches me the importance of being still and praying for wisdom and guidance. Logically I understand this idea, but practically it has never become a habit that I have successfully incorporated into my life. The idea of physically sitting for any period, doing nothing but reflecting, seemed about as enjoyable as an eight-hour flight surrounded by screaming babies. I knew about meditation and have had friends participate in weekend silent retreats and year-long spiritual direction programs, but I knew, in my current state, that these would be too big a leap for me. My journey towards meditation and mindfulness began as I was experiencing a full-on mind storm, sitting on my back deck. My parents, possibly through some kind of premonition, had given me their bench swing when they moved to a condominium the previous year. I had grudgingly accepted it, loaded it into my friend's truck, and reassembled it in my backyard where it had sat unoccupied for over eleven months. The only time I had touched it was to move it as I cut my lawn. Fast forward to the present and I will proclaim that this has become my favourite place to be between the months of May and October, to reflect, connect and reset.

My realization of the magic of the swing did not happen right away, though there were brief moments of strange insights that bubbled up almost from day one. My first day on the swing was one of stress and downward spiral. I created the above-described mind storm from a few "coffee connects" that had not been very encouraging and ongoing concerns over my wife's illness, which was still undiagnosed and troubling. The tension and anxiety in our house were palpable, and my mind was frequently skidding out of control. I was tired from a week of restless sleep and I just needed some time for myself, a unique experience for a highly extroverted person. I wandered into the back with a book I had meant to start a few months ago, sat on the swing and while reading slowly fell asleep.

I'm not sure how long I slept—most likely less than a half an hour—but I woke up to an amazing and strange discovery. As I opened my eyes, I saw what seemed like an old Disney cartoon from my childhood. It stunned me to see two rabbits, chipmunks and multiple birds frolicking in my small backyard while being serenaded by the wind, the rustle of the leaves in the trees and the buzz of the bees. Now I know this sounds strange and not typically what you might find in the suburbs, but somehow, in that moment, I found myself transported into a place of pause and peace. While in this momentary space of bliss, I had my first big insight about the power of pause. Nothing had changed in my circumstances except that a pause had allowed me to see beyond them. When I arrived in this place of pause, it allowed access to the fuller experience around me and led me to a place of humour (old Disney songs playing in my head), beauty (surrounded by and reminded of nature) and an overall deeper sense of spirituality and connectedness. It felt like I had discovered the truth of what S.A. Jefferson-Wright once said: "Serenity is not freedom from the storm but peace amid the storm." In that moment I had experienced what I would later know as mindfulness, a mental state achieved by focusing one's awareness on the present moment while calmly acknowledging and accepting one's feelings, thoughts, and bodily sensations.

I believe that regardless of one's faith tradition, we all have had snippets of what many would call mindfulness. Those moments when we are connected to both ourselves and something bigger than our-selves. Think about a time when you felt most at peace. When did you have a deep sense of gratefulness, joy and amazement? When were you surprised with a moment of what some people would call "flow"? Take five minutes, think about that time, and unearth those mindfulness moments. What were you doing? What were you seeing? Who were you with? What were you feeling? I believe all of us have had at least a few of these moments; however, in our driven world, we often lose sight of them as they are buried deeper and deeper under the stress and pressures of everyday life. Reaching this state will not eliminate the stress and pressures that are being placed on you, but I believe it will increase your ability to see beyond the immediate storm and experience peace within it. The richness of this experience on the swing led me to investigate ways in which I could increase and repeat this event. This search led me to a deeper appreciation for the practice of meditation.

I am definitely not an expert in meditation (see the SBS website for books and other tools related to the topic), and none of my fam-ily could have predicted that I would end up spending a minimum of two fifteen-minute sessions meditating every day. That being said, this habit has been one of the most impactful shifts in my life. I highly recommend it to enhance your ability to be "in the pause." As I have strengthened my practice, three helpful insights for me have been (1) to pick a consistent time and place, (2) to disconnect completely, and (3) to leverage simple, helpful tools.

The first insight is the importance of finding a consistent physi-cal space and, if possible, time to pause. Now this doesn't mean you should go out right now and buy a swing for your back lawn, although for some of you this might be exactly what you need. Most teach-ers in meditation, mindfulness and spiritual direction recommend finding a quiet, consistent location to strengthen your pause muscle. Although my place was a swing, other friends have picked locations such as their favourite walking path, while driving in the car alone, or a corner of their basement. One friend who lives in a very busy household has discovered the only available place of calm is while they are in the washroom (restroom, water closet, etc. for our global readers). As for finding a consistent time, there are a lot of studies that suggest that blocking off a regular time enables greater success in achieving a habit. When that time is will depend upon your personal situation, when your energy is the highest. I am personally more of a morning person and like to get up before the rest of my family. Over the past three years I have slowly increased my pause practice to 45 minutes every morning, beginning between 6:30 and 7 a.m. and now incorporating mediation, stretching and journaling. I have also recently added a 10-to-15-minute mini-meditation in the afternoon to boost my pause power. Some of you may be night owls, while others might find that midday walks not only give you a chance to pause but also provide a needed refresh in the middle of your busy day.

Wherever and whenever you choose, the second suggestion is to disconnect completely, no music, audiobooks, etc. Just you. One of my favourite visuals to help me disconnect and fully enter a period of pause—an image that someone else shared with me—is to imagine myself floating down a lazy river, being carried by the current and observing everything around me. When I first heard this idea, I was immediately transported back to my childhood and a small water park in the city where I grew up. I remembered moments when I was lying on my back with my ears in the water staring up at the sky watching the clouds go by while hearing muffled sounds of laughter. It made me think about how, as time goes by and we fully get more deeply influenced by the circumstances around us, we slowly lose the clearer perspectives that we have as a child. Blocking out everything and observing your surroundings strengthens your pause muscles. As you start this process one thing you will quickly realize is that your mind does not stop churning worries, ideas and distractions. Two simple exercises have been helpful for me when this occurs:

- Acknowledge the thought, and say "thank you, not now." It shocked me the first time I used this technique how simply and powerfully it allowed me to let go in the moment.
- Returning to the image of lying on my back and watching the

clouds, recognize that thoughts are simply clouds passing through our minds and that we can watch them approach and then float away.

Also helpful in enabling my ability to pause has been finding and leveraging a few simple, accessible tools to help support my development in mindfulness and mediation. Two things that have been foundational to my progress are (1) my daily meditation app and (2) my daily SNAP reminder. The meditation app that I use is called CALM. There are tons of tools within the app including a simple 10-minute daily meditation; this is the one I use regularly, having just passed my 1,000th session with my longest streak being 101 days. Besides the daily session there are also more specific and longer mediations for sleep, to handle various emotions, for mental fitness, and for children. There are many other apps out there including HeadSpace, Abide and Aura that provide a variety of guided meditations to strengthen deeper self-awareness and mindfulness. Each app also now includes trackers and the ability to partner with friends and family to increase the likelihood of building the habit.

The second thing, which I added six months after starting meditation, is a simple reminder on my phone that comes up at noon every day. The reminder, created by Ian Cron, adapted with a bit of my thinking, and making use of Byron Katie's model, simply asks me to SNAP:

- S—stop and take three deep breaths;
- N—notice, look around and just observe (what are you seeing, what do you feel?);
- A—ask (self-inquiry): what am I believing right now? Is it true? Who would I be if I let go of this belief and believe something different that is truer?
- P—pivot or praise: pivot to a truer belief, praise or thanks for the positive truth in the moment.

SNAP helps me reinforce the learning from morning meditation and strengthen my self-awareness.

Mindfulness and meditation have really helped me to increase my ability to "be" in pause. "Being" is that place of letting go in the storm's midst, that sense of floating down the lazy river, that ability to be fully present in the moment. When we are fully present, we "see" so much more. It is like finally finding your lost keys when you have been searching for ages with no success. It is only when you slow down that you see that they are, and have always been, right in front of you. As I recognized the energy surges in me and remembered to pause, I saw a pathway to channel my energy towards a more positive response. In that moment, I chose to ELOPE.

Take some time to reflect on the things you have just read around the power of pause and consider the following to empower your pause:

- What resonated most as "true" for you within this section? Why? What most challenges and/or churns within you? Why?
- Select one exercise to strengthen your ability to pause and capture the insights. Are you learning in the pause?

Choosing to ELOPE

Over the past several years, I have noticed a trend of couples choosing to escape the stress and energy spikes of a big, formal wedding ceremony and instead elope to destination weddings with their closest friends and family. By removing the stress of these complicated traditions and having a more intimate ceremony, they then return refreshed and released, often to enjoy a celebratory party with a broader community. Interestingly, Merriam-Webster has changed the definition of "elope" from "running away" to "shifting towards." I love that change and having witnessed both scenarios, it got me thinking that this is the pathway that has enabled me to connect with and channel my energy to a more positive use and impact. I also recognize that this decision is something that we "choose" to do. Viktor Frankl once said, "Between the stimulus and response there's a space, and within that space lies the power to choose our response. In the response lies our growth and our freedom." When I strengthen my ability to pause, I enable the power of choice through a pathway I call ELOPE.

- E > recognize and name the **Energy.**
- L > experience it (yourself, the situation, others involved) through the eyes of **Love,** empathy, gratefulness, mercy and compassion.
- O > through the eyes of love we enable **Openness,** curiosity and wonder.
- P > in this state of openness we are able to be more **Present** in this moment.
- E > when we are truly present, we can more fully **Engage** and connect with ourselves and others.

Like a couple who choose to elope, deciding to shift towards a place of more intimacy and connectedness, when I follow this pathway personally I shift towards a deeper level both in myself and with others. This deeper wisdom is the place of "flow" that I described earlier and always enables better choices, decisions, responses and experiences. This is also an entry path to unveiling safe brave spaces.

ENERGY
Recognize and name the energy.

Earlier we spent a lot of time fleshing out the importance of, and ways to become more aware of, energy. Leveraging my newly discovered personal Doppler radar, I was strengthening my ability to sense its arrival and the impact it has on me. This is a combination of body work, sensing the energy shift, and mind work, naming the energy. This helps us identify what is happening, how it is making us feel and what it is making us want to do. The E in ELOPE is all about noticing and naming the energy shift that is occurring, a shift which often hinders us in activating our full selves. Historically, this has been a place where I have sometimes stalled or been carried away with the storm. To shift to a more positive outcome, I needed to shift from my head to my heart; I needed to see through the eyes of Love.

LOVE

Experience it (yourself, the situation, others involved) through the eyes of love, gratitude, mercy, and compassion.

Love is a complicated word that will immediately send some people to places of warmth and joy and others to uncomfortable and even sometimes difficult places. The Merriam-Webster dictionary defines love as "a strong affection for another arising out of kinship or personal ties; affection based on admiration, benevolence, or common interests and/or unselfish loyal and benevolent concern for the good of another." Although I think this is a good definition, within this context I prefer the term *Agape Love*, which is a Greco-Christian term referring to "the highest form of love, charity" and "the love of God for humans and of humans for God." Depending on your tradition you might replace God with something else; however, the essence is a love that is bigger, connected to others and something beyond ourselves, and yet including ourselves. When we shift to our heart and experience this form of love, we experience "flow," including a sense of peace, joy and freedom.

Whatever we call this or relate this to, I believe each of us has experienced it at least once in our lifetime. For me personally these experiences include witnessing the birth of my children, the day of my marriage (we didn't elope but we did have a smaller, more intimate gathering!) and delivering newspapers at the age of twelve in the silence and peace of the very early morning. In each of these moments I felt separate and yet totally connected. Tapping into my heart, my desire to love and to be love is my entry point towards accessing my fullest self. I knew how I felt within these situations. The challenge was how I could more consistently make the leap from E to L. As with everything, this ability requires a few excellent exercises and practice, practice, practice. Two areas of focus that have been most helpful for me to see through the eyes of love are acceptance and gratefulness.

Acceptance is about recognizing that over our lifetimes we have become programmed by our experiences and our innate and learned responses to those experiences. The most important habit that I have learned to shift me towards this mindset is to smile and laugh at the predictable arrival of my reactions. Parker J. Palmer stated, "I now know myself to be a person of weakness and strength, liability and giftedness, darkness and light. I know that to be whole means to reject none of it, but to embrace all of it."

Becoming more aware of the patterns and triggers that ignite my energy boosts, acknowledging their arrival and accepting them as part of my growth process is freeing. This acknowledgement and acceptance naturally moved me to the second step of gratitude. Seeing and understanding the power of eloping reinforced that acceptance was a critical step and the sooner I could do this, the quicker I would move towards gratefulness.

Gratefulness is about "seeing the gift in each moment." It begins with being grateful for this enhanced awareness of yourself and how energy shifts impact you and your ability to choose how you respond. Greater awareness sparks curiosity and recognition that each moment is an opportunity to learn and grow. This awareness of the "gift" helps me be grateful for the "giver." That could be me or others. A simple technique that has helped me quickly move towards a state of gratefulness is called "Flip the script," and requires one to shift the question from what is happening *to* me, to what is happening *for* me. Over the next 24 hours, switch out this one word and see what happens. If you are a "mind" person like me and you need to further strengthen your heart muscle, here are three easy and more in-depth exercises for you to try—three simple ways to cultivate a daily gratitude practice:

- Keep a gratitude journal. Spend five minutes each day writing three things that you're grateful for in your life right now.
- Write a gratitude letter to someone. Sending the letter is optional. The mere act of putting positive thoughts on paper can help shift your cognitive processes.
- Commit to expressing gratitude to someone at least once a day.

A key character in Antoine de Saint-Exupéry's book *The Little Prince* declares, "Here is my secret. It is very simple: it is only with the heart that one can see rightly. What is essential is invisible to the eye." Seeing through the lens of love allows us to begin accepting ourselves, the gift in the moment and the giver. This perspective enables a deep sense of gratefulness, which evokes a deeper sense of openness toward the entire experience.

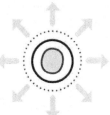

OPENNESS
Through the eyes of love we enable openness, curiosity, and wonder.

Openness is about seeing beyond the moment, like zooming out with a camera to take in a broader and more inclusive picture. A therapist once helped me understand that when I step back, I can get a fuller view of both my own and others' journeys. From this broader perspective we often discover that although we/they may not be as far down the road as we might wish, we can see where we/they began, and often are surprised to realize the distance already travelled. This greater awareness releases a deeper sense of curiosity, empathy, graciousness and appreciation.

Our inner curiosity promotes a desire to understand what is behind the energy that is bubbling up inside and coming towards us. Stephen Covey, in his book *The Seven Habits of Effective People*, describes this as "seeking to understand before being understood." Saki chi Toyoda, the Japanese industrialist, inventor, and founder of Toyota Industries, transformed organizational culture when he developed the "Five Whys" technique in the 1930s. This technique became a primary component of the organization's "go and see" philosophy, which promotes "seek first to understand" ideals. The method is remarkably simple: when a problem occurs, you drill down to its root cause by asking "Why?" five times. Then, when a counter-measure becomes apparent, you follow it through to prevent the issue from recurring. "Five Whys" helps shift us towards greater openness by requiring us to deepen our understanding prior to trying to resolve or respond to a situation.

Besides this technique, three simple approaches that have also helped me to strengthen my sense of curiosity are (1) to see through my child's eye; (2) "tell me more"; and (3) to shift from position to experience.

Seeing through my child's eye is simply asking myself what four-year-old Greg would see. I have a picture of my four-year-old self posted in my office and saved on my phone, as a touchstone to help open up my curiosity. At this age I know I was much freer of biases, expectations and fears and more open to the possibilities of the moment. It is amazing how quickly I return to that space by looking into my eyes in this picture. The second process, "tell me more," is a slight tweak to the "Five Whys." I have found that requesting more information enhances openness where asking "why" sometimes creates an environment of doubt which can diminish openness. The last approach, shifting from position to experience, enables the ability to step back and see more broadly. If we try to understand position, we often miss out on the most important aspects of intention and influence, which are discovered by inquiring about experience. Asking what experiences helped you reach that position or conclusion provides an opportunity to discover hidden insights and ideas.

I have found that when I use these techniques, I experience the innate by-products of empathy, graciousness and appreciation. As I expand my openness, I build greater empathy, defined as "the ability to understand and share the feelings of another." Empathy builds emotional and intellectual bridges (mind and heart melds) within me and with others, resulting in graciousness, defined as "a generosity of spirit and kindness" and appreciation, a feeling or expression of admiration, approval and gratitude. Like a flywheel, as I strengthen these attributes, I further expand my openness. Within this expanded openness, I become more present in the moment.

PRESENT
In this state of openness, we are able to be present to this moment.

Being fully present is an amazing place to discover, and it is often very hard to describe. I have stumbled into this state most often when I am experiencing extreme levels of either joy or sorrow. In these moments I experienced a deep sense of stillness. It felt as though the frame of my life froze and I became completely focused on connecting with someone else and/or something bigger. It felt as if everything else faded away, including emotions and distractions. When I found myself in these states of full presence, in both joyous and sorrowful situations, I felt a sense of peace, joy, safety, gratefulness and wonder. What I saw was usually a slow-motion movement of wind, light and sound and what I sensed was a level of confidence that "all was good" and an encouragement to be calm.

The moments of joy that released this sense of being fully present for me were the birth of my children and marriage to my spouse. I have described the birth of my children to many friends as the time the world stopped. With both my daughter and my son, I was in the birthing room and as they arrived, it was as though a master photographer used their lens to blur the surrounding room and just focus on my wife, my newborn and me. I remained in this state until the nurse placed my child in my arms and said "Mr. Smith, meet your new daughter/son." I had the same experience at my wedding as my wife walked down the aisle with her parents. The focus was on the two of us, everything else blurred and the sounds faded until we took each other's hands.

The moments of sorrow and fear were equally impacting. Early in the book I described a near-death experience at age sixteen. Although I was a relatively well-behaved youth, one summer I had gone to a party in a local park and consumed too much alcohol. A desire to fit in and to be liked impacted my judgement, which resulted in me being severely impaired. Enter a bully who thought it would be fun to spin me around and push me down an embankment. Within a few brief minutes I found myself lying face down in a river with no strength or ability to move. In that moment I experienced the same sense that I described above. Although I knew I was dying I was at peace. I felt "seen," focused on the moment and sensed that "all would be good." Lost in that moment I heard someone call out, "Smitty, what are you doing?" and felt someone grab the back of my shirt and throw me up on the bank. My best friend, who was equally inebriated, somehow saw me fall and had stumbled down the bank to save me.

The second situation came years later in the Dominican Republic when a few friends from my work and our daughters had gone on a mission trip to build houses. On the second-last day we went cliff jumping, and I swallowed some water on one of my jumps. Little did I know that I had ingested some amoebas, which by the following morning had begun attacking my body. By 10 a.m. I had collapsed and was convulsing on the steps of my hotel with my daughter screaming for help. Fortunately, my other travelling companions were near; the father of one of them lived in the town and was the founder of the charity. They quickly threw me in our van and rushed to the American clinic. During the trip, I continued to drift in and out of focus. All I can remember is one woman praying for me and the others yelling at my friend to drive quicker. Arriving at the clinic, they rushed me to an examination room where I once again experienced this sense of being fully present. Lying on the bed I remember seeing the wind from a window gently dance with the sheer curtain. I experienced a wave of peacefulness during this storm of illness. I remember hearing a woman's voice ask where I was from. When I answered Canada, she said "So am I, I'm from Elmira" (a small town one hour from where I grew up). How crazy is it that in the middle of the Dominican Republic, in a small city, the nurse who was taking care of me was from home! This sense of peace deepened as she told me it was good that I collapsed here as they were familiar with the symptoms and had already begun treatment.

In each of the above situations, I now recognize two common themes that are part of the ELOPE model, including feeling a deep sense of love and gratitude, letting go of all the things I couldn't control, and being open to what was in the moment. This deeper pause and presence provided the key to engage and connect to my inner wisdom and with those around me.

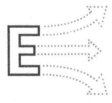

ENGAGE
When we are truly present, we can more fully engage and connect with ourselves and with others.

A common definition of being engaged is "being proactively committed to, embedded with, connected to something or someone." It is probably one of the most overused words of the past twenty years. It has many interpretations and excites some as much as it annoys others. For the purpose of ELOPE, I'd like to define engagement as a state of full connection to our whole selves and those around us. When we are fully connected, we open up complete awareness of and access to the other parts that haven't yet developed to their full potential. I have begun to understand that as we ELOPE, we release within ourselves our dependency on the one part of us that has often been overused—in my case the mind—and access the other parts, in my case my body and heart. I mentioned earlier that for me, my go-to place in most situations is my mind. I am definitely a "think first" person and I believe that this has been an important strength that has helped me to be successful. For some of you, your first move is "doing," as an "action person" who may later consider the feeling and logic centres. Others are more "heart"-driven and go to the feelings of themselves and others first before thinking through a situation and/ or moving to action. All these innate first-step approaches are unique strengths that each of us brings to each situation and are accentuated by the surges of energy that we either create or receive. The greater truth that I am discovering is that full engagement comes when we access all three parts of us, the head, the heart and the body. Later in the book I will share some frameworks I have discovered to support both unveiling and activating my fuller self.

With this discovery we reveal a greater truth and wisdom, which some call the soul, the gut, or what perhaps is best described by the Sanskrit term "Chitta." Chitta is defined as the unconscious store-house or reservoir of all impressions. Think of this as the holding area for your fullest self, your mind, heart, body and soul, within which are stored your desires, memories, sensations, feelings, emotions and experiences. It is also a place where somehow we are connected to others and, I also believe, to a greater source. In my tradition we represent it as the Holy Spirit; for others it might be a oneness, nature, and so on.

When I ELOPE, I can more regularly and easily access this inner wisdom or Chitta, which always enhances my personal potential through better decision-making, creativity and relationship building. Having greater and more consistent access to this wisdom better equipped me to strengthen both my personal safe and brave muscles. In the next chapter, I'll share in more details about my journey and some additional tools and discoveries I picked up on the trip.

This evolved state of wisdom within me also enhanced my desire and abilities to connect with others on a deeper level. The energy disruptions that occurred when I collided with others became positive accelerators for my one-on-one relationships and within my broader communities. Equipped with the learnings from ELOPE, I was better prepared to enable and create safe brave spaces in these interactions. With this framework I replayed critical moments in my past where I had innately followed this pathway, one of those being the Toys "R" Us experience I shared earlier. Applying the ELOPE framework to that story, I discovered that:

- E—I recognized and named the **energy** spike while in the lobby: fear and anxiety.
- L—through the lens of **love** I accepted it as simply energy and was grateful for the positive side of it and the ability to channel it.
- O—love **opened** me to the possibilities beyond the moment to shift from anxiety to confidence.
- P—becoming more **present** to the truths of my knowledge and my preparedness, I could visualize the channeling of my energy in a positive, impactful way.
- E—this allowed me to **engage** with my whole self, tapping into my confidence, my experiences, my deeper self, and enabled safe brave space, freeing me towards my fullest potential and as a result strengthening my connection to those to whom I was presenting.

When I rewound these past "tapes," I saw the same pattern every time that I had somehow positively managed an energy spike. If this worked with energy spikes, I wondered whether it would also work on the other end of the spectrum, with energy lulls and drains. This question arose one morning after a somewhat distracted meditation, driven by exhaustion created by poor sleep and challenging dreams that had left me with no energy and a sense of discouragement and sadness. I couldn't really put my finger on what had placed me in this state, but I knew I was in an energy valley with a "leak" that was taking me still lower. In this state of mind, I applied the ELOPE framework and discovered that it was equally helpful for these situations:

- E—I recognized where I was, low and leaking **energy**, discouraged and sad.
- L—Through the lens of **love**, I accepted and saw the gift in the

moment. Low energy forces me to be more still.

- O—this recognition helped me **open** my perspective, shifting from sadness and doubt to a sense of curiosity for what I might discover in the stillness.
- P—this strengthened the pause and helped me be more **present** to my wisdom.
- E—**engaged** with and connected to my deeper self, I recognized that often it is in this state that I most grow and deepen my empathy, which strengthens my ability to enable safe brave spaces.

Later in the book I'll share more details of how I have been applying ELOPE in my relationships and within my communities, along with some additional tools and discoveries gained along the way in my search for safe brave spaces.

Take some time to reflect on the things you have just read around the idea of ELOPE. Capture your thoughts around the following questions and consider choosing to ELOPE in a couple of situations:

- What resonated most as "true" for you within this section? Why? What most challenges and/or churns within you? Why?
- Consider choosing to ELOPE:
  - Review the ELOPE model.
  - Apply—Think about a recent conflict/energy disruption and review it through the filter of ELOPE. What would you change and/or maintain in your response?

- o Leverage the ELOPE model and reflection guide when you next sense a surge of negative energy. Pause and walk through the model and then capture any new learnings and insights.
- Record the patterns and insights you are noticing.

3. The Safe Brave Spaces Journey

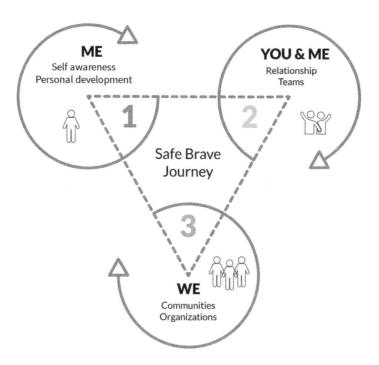

Having defined the state of safe brave spaces (which I will occasionally abbreviate as "SBS" to save space and avoid repetition) and discovered the critical equipment for my journey, the importance of energy, the power of pause, and the ability to ELOPE, I was better prepared to create the map for my journey. As I began charting the path, I quickly realized that to reach full potential in this journey to safe brave spaces it …

1. Starts within ME—enabling safe brave spaces within myself;
2. Accelerates between YOU & ME—enabling safe brave spaces within my one-to-one relationships; and
3. Flourishes through WE—enabling safe brave spaces within my broader communities.

Although I believe that the journey to fully releasing safe brave spaces starts with me, I also recognize that the stages of this growth are not linear and, much like the process of gaining insight into the four sources of energy, are highly integrated. The beauty of this integration is that as we advance in one stage it naturally enables expansion in the others. Before we dive into the actual journey it might help by fleshing out each of these stages.

Safe Brave Spaces Starts within ME

Anyone who has flown is familiar with the safety training prior to takeoff. Over time, many of us ignore these presentations as they are already deeply seared into our brains; however, one of the most important points they cover is that, in an incident, the first thing you need to do is put on your own mask before trying to help others. This guidance runs true in all things, including the journey towards safe brave spaces. To be equipped for the broader journey it is important to put on the right equipment and gain the knowledge needed to help us build our own safe and brave muscles before supporting others. This important first step will significantly increase the likelihood of enabling safe brave spaces in your one-on-one relationships and in the communities of which you are a member. The ME chapter will provide some insights, ideas and tools to help advance safe brave spaces within yourself.

Safe Brave Spaces Accelerates between YOU & ME

Beginning by working within yourself is critical, but everything happens in-between, as the saying goes. There are very few of us—if any—who don't ever interact with others. We bring our unique energy and ideas to these interactions, something which naturally creates disruptions both within ourselves and between one another. These disruptions can be positive or negative and can increase or decrease our individual and collective safe brave space. In each of these situations we have the opportunity to understand, value and channel this collective energy towards enhancing our relationships, our potential, and our safe brave space (both individually and collectively). Later in the book we will explore YOU & ME and will provide some insights, ideas and tools to help advance SBS in your one-to-one relationship.

SBS Flourishes through WE

As we expand beyond the one-to-one relationship things can get even trickier. Imagine multiple and varying levels of energy, ideas and experience coming together in one place at one time. It has the potential to become either a super storm or a super safe brave spaces surge. I am certain that everyone of us has at one time experienced, at least to some degree, each of these situations. In a super storm, we experience heightened anxiety, fear, frustration and ultimately an energy drain or explosion. In a super SBS surge, we enter a rhythm, a flow which heightens excitement, joy and a sense of peace at the same time and ultimately restores and advances energy.

One last thought before we dive into the journey. Within each of these phases I myself am still a work in progress. I've discovered that when I reach what I thought was the end of my trip, there is a whole new horizon beyond the original destination. I am convinced that the journey is a life journey, with some setbacks, but also with more joy, peace and freedom that I could have ever imagined when I stepped off the curb and began.

ME, YOU & ME, and WE are Activated through Knowing, Growing, Letting Go and Showing Up

In the introduction to this book I shared the observation that, as with a physical workout, to build our safe and brave muscles we need to build and follow a plan. This plan needs to be simple and applicable across all stages of the journey and build upon each stage to create momentum, rather like intermeshing gears. Change happens and the best-laid plans almost always have to be tweaked and adjusted, so I have needed more of a framework or a sandbox, rather than a locked-in process, allowing lots of space to shift as I move along this journey. My ability and decision to ELOPE enabled the workout routine and included four consistent steps: Knowing, Growing, Letting Go and Showing Up.

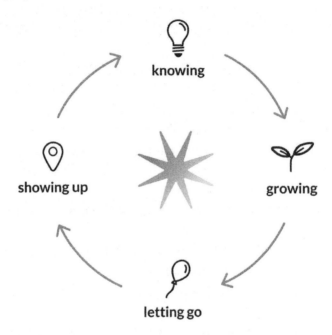

Knowing is about caringly and honestly exploring and understanding our current shape and state.

Growing is about investing in, accepting, loving, trusting and expanding this understanding.

Letting Go is about forgiveness, forgetting and freeing us from the patterns and responses that inhibit us; and

Showing Up is about preparing for and leveraging the learning and awareness to enable safe brave spaces in every moment.

As I reflected on how this routine supported my journey towards safe brave spaces, I quickly realized that Knowing and Growing are key to strengthening our safe muscles and safe spaces as they deepen awareness, confidence and understanding. Letting Go and Showing

Up are also critical as they spark curiosity, courage, openness and connectivity. The beauty of this framework is that each step is interconnected; the smallest movement of the one moves all the others. When we combine the concepts of ME, YOU & ME, and WE with Knowing, Growing, Letting Go and Showing Up we see the possibilities of momentum and release the fullest potential of safe brave spaces.

Safe Brave Spaces Starts within ME

The first step in my journey towards safe brave spaces was to put on my (metaphorical) oxygen mask. Many of us often find ourselves low on oxygen, short of breath, inhibiting both our personal impact and the success of others. Steven Covey describes this situation using a different metaphor by recommending that we need to continually "sharpen our saw," as it takes a lot more work to cut through something with a dull blade than a sharp one. Unfortunately, in our often turbulent current world, finding the time to focus on ME is not an easy task, and it often takes a serious setback to prioritize ourselves. For me this occurred in the summer of 2016, amid my personal crash, shared earlier in the book.

During that personal storm, as I began to more consistently choose to ELOPE, I found that I became more aware in more situations, especially when I was spending more time with others. Being "more aware" meant that I was more curious and open to what others had to say, even if what they said was misaligned with my current thinking or state of mind. The initial insight that the journey towards safe brave spaces "Starts within ME" came when a good friend helped me reframe my current situation by suggesting that I see what they described as the "gift in the moment." Rather than focusing on what was happening *to* me, she suggested that I re-frame it to consider what was happening *for* me. She provoked me to take this unique opportunity to explore ME and to rediscover what was important to me, what gifts I had been given in my life so far (and how I had used them), what I wanted to do now, and where and with whom I wanted to do it. As she spoke those words my heart literally skipped, my energy spiked (mostly positive but combined with a smidge of anxiety), and I instantly knew this was the first fork in the road toward a fresh way of thinking and being.

> *Be yourself; everyone else is already taken.*
> —Oscar Wilde.

> *Today you are you, that is truer than true.*
> *There is no one alive who is youer than you.*
> —Dr. Seuss

The above two quotations fueled my exploration of ME by reminding me I have a unique perspective and that I am the best one to uncover it. I quickly discovered that the path to rediscovering oneself is not an even, easy road but a windy, hilly, sunny, blustery, lonely and fulfilling trip. It provides much excitement and joy, some pain as you work and shift through uncomfortable self-doubts and biases, and deepening clarity that leads to a greater sense of peace and freedom. Many traditions confirm that the pathway to personal freedom and personal growth is enhanced through challenges and difficulty and (as the Zen saying captures the matter) "the only way to it is through it."

At the time I began this journey both my safe and brave muscles were suffering from severe atrophy and without the support of a small group of friends I'm not sure I would have been able to take those first few steps. As noted earlier, I first needed to enhance my personal safety through knowing and growing ME. I called this my "ME Search stage," as it was really about taking a deep look at who I was, what I believed, and where I wished to contribute.

Knowing ME involved reflecting upon and capturing my strengths, values, purpose, passions, fears and biases. Once I had completed this step, I entered the Growing ME phase, which involved gaining deeper insight, love and acceptance of myself. These two steps strengthened both my awareness and my confidence, rebuilding the foundation and beginning to re-establish a sense of personal safety. As my safe muscles strengthened, I was better able to take the steps to enhance my brave muscles.

Becoming braver required me to learn to Let Go, especially of the things that impeded me from accepting and trusting myself. These included self-judgment, doubt, and fear—key contributors to what I earlier described as my mind storms. As I learned to let go, I more consistently Showed Up as my fullest self, resulting in a more meaningful contribution and also in personal growth.

Knowing Me

Knowing Me was a process of peeling back my personal onion to discover the sweet core that was ME. It is the first step I needed to take to build my safe muscles and involved caringly and honestly exploring and understanding my current shape and state. Looking back from where I find myself today, I recognize that at the beginning of this journey my perception and understanding of myself was very limited, and I had reached a point where, like a person with a slowly forming cataract, what I thought was clear was actually cloudy and distorted. Rather than start from scratch, I first began by "mining ME," by investigating what I already knew about myself.

Fortunately, over my career I have completed several assessments and exercises that would help inform this process. I began by spending a few hours digging through boxes buried deep in my basement and searching through hard drives on my computer to find these various reports that might shine a light on ME. I created a "ME Wall" in my basement and began capturing insights and observations using Post-it notes and print-outs, putting them in the buckets *My Gifts and Strengths* (aka *What I Bring*); *My Values and My Passions* (aka *What I Care About*); *My Unique Approach* (aka *How I Work Best*); and *My Blockers, Triggers and Truths* (aka *What gets in my Way*). (For those of you who lack an empty wall, I have recently discovered the app "Post-it," which can serve as your personal and virtual wall.) An exercise which sparked some ad-

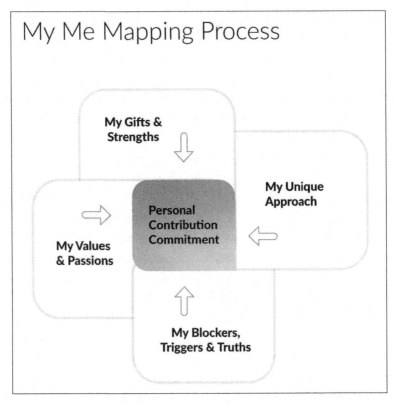

My Me Mapping Process

My Gifts & Strengths

My Unique Approach

Personal Contribution Commitment

My Values & Passions

My Blockers, Triggers & Truths

ditional exploration is a fairly well-known model called "Ikigai." This model, which was first documented in Japan in the 1970s, requires you to answer four simple questions to help unveil your purpose. My ME Wall work and the questions from Ikigai provided the foundation for what would become my ME Mapping process.

My ME Mapping process quickly helped me zoom out to gain a wider perspective of what it was to Be ME. One build to the Ikigai model that I found helpful was to add a fifth question: *What do you value?* Often what you love, you also value. However, this created a slightly different perspective and produced some additional insights for me. With this foundational work completed, I was better informed to expand my understanding and frame three important guideposts: *My Strengths, Abilities and Gifts; My Values;* and *My Personal Purpose.* These three areas are foundational to me knowing, accepting and believing in my unique contribution. Trust and confidence in this contribution is at the heart of my being and feeling safe.

Meaningful Moments and Gifts Discovery

As I reviewed my ME Wall, I realized I had a clearer understanding of some buckets compared to others. In determining Values, Purpose and Strengths/Gifts, I was fortunate to be able to draw on a process I had led at Campbell's in the early 2000s called Authentic Leadership, where, in partnership with Wayne and Mike from an organization called Pursuit, we created an amazing program to support the organizational vision of "Extraordinary, Authentic Nourishment for All." The internal expression of that vision drove us to create an innovative journey for all managers to discover and release their unique purpose, values, gifts and talents individually and collectively as we strived to bring this purposeful organizational vision to life. The importance of this work and the power of transformation that occurred within me personally and within each leader at Campbell's was beyond what any of us could have dreamed when we first declared our intentions. There are now hundreds of leaders helping to release the potential of their organizations through their people, who themselves were transformed through this program. As I reviewed my original work that was first created over 15 years ago, I quickly saw that it was still relevant and applicable to my current state. With this in mind, I began refreshing my work using three simple exercises that had most contributed to my earlier self-discovery and articulation of my values, purpose and gifts.

My Meaningful Experiences and Gifts Journal

This first step, My Meaningful Experiences and Gifts Journal, requires you to capture, over a two to three-week period, insights in various areas, reviewing them to find themes and patterns, and then discussing them with a coach or friend. Throughout this book we have been talking about the importance of energy and this idea of an inner wisdom or reservoir that stores so much insight within each of us. The power of intention is an amazing thing. Just declaring a desire to mine for these experiences seems to open up forgotten channels back to the reservoir. As we tap into our ability to ELOPE and use other techniques to slow down and pause, we strengthen our connection to experiences that hold the most meaning for each of us.

Meaningful experiences are events that reflect very satisfying results and that brought you a sense of joy, fulfillment and a feeling that you were at your very best. These moments may not reflect your biggest accomplishments; they might instead reflect your deepest sense of satisfaction. Folks who are spiritual often reflect on times when they are in "flow" with the spirit. These moments may also involve challenging circumstances that upon later reflection you recognize as unique and powerful breakthroughs. Extending this exercise over a period of at least a few weeks also frees us to feel unburdened by the pressure to see and allows insights and memories to bubble up from within. As these memories arise, in a journal of your choosing (either paper or electronic)—

1. Capture the specific details of the moments. Where were you? What were you doing? Who was with you? How were you feeling?
2. Think about the moment and capture your insights, guided by the following questions:
   • What was most meaningful for you?
   • What was most meaningful for others you were with?
   • What are the common themes and insights that best describe what activities and/or interests you love and are drawn to?

After a few weeks of capturing these experiences, the second step is the identification of supporting gifts, abilities and skills that enable your meaningful experiences. I am convinced that each of us has natural gifts; things that you just see, just sense or just know; abilities that have always been a part of you. We also have learned abilities and skills that we have gained because of the unique experiences in our lives; these support and build upon our gifts. As no individual's experience is exactly like another's, each of us has a unique perspective and learning path. Specific situations have offered opportunities to apply your gifts and abilities in a way that provided unique value to you, others and the communities you have supported. These gifts and abilities, evidenced in your meaningful experiences, are easily identified by:

- **Reflecting** on each of your meaningful experiences, and
- **Capturing** what gifts, learned abilities and skills you brought to those situations.

One last step worth capturing as you review these experiences are the patterns around "how best I worked." Earlier, while talking about energy, I shared that my earliest insights came from a tool called the Kolbe Index. This was a very specific assessment that helped me identify how best I worked, in particular when I was striving for results and decisions. Categorized by the tool as a "Quick Start" and, secondarily, a "Fact Finder," I discovered that I innately maximize my personal energy and results through taking risks, engaging with others and then validating with facts. Each of us is unique in how we problem-solve and take action to maximize our personal effectiveness and the effectiveness with which we work with others. Some of us require more detail, some are great at organizing and structuring information and processes; some of us like to drive change while others prefer to support. Capture what is your best way, a way that gives you energy and enables your personal effectiveness. Tools such as DISC, Hogan, Instincts, and MBTI are also helpful in uncovering the answer to this important question.

You have now completed the first important phase in deepening your understanding of you. We can add all the above information to your ME Wall and leverage it to help inform the next two exercises, identification of your core values and passions and creation of a personal contribution commitment statement.

Personal Values

Having a better understanding of what has been and is meaningful to me, combined with clarity around what unique gifts, abilities and skills I bring to the world, is an important place to start as it helps build confidence and focus on potential areas of both impact and contribution. This awareness is an important cornerstone to strengthening safe brave spaces within ME. The second area of focus, **personal values**, is equally important. These are your "touchstones" for decisions and actions that are critical as you begin your journey. There are several wonderful processes to help an individual flesh out core guiding values, and the previous work around meaningful experiences will most likely help inform this stage of self-discovery.

The most in-depth of these processes that have supported my own journey was created by Pursuit Inc. and was included in the Authentic Leadership program at Campbell's. Within this process (which I loved so much I later became certified to support others), you identify not only your **Top 10 Values** but your **Driver Value** (what is critical for you to have present and honoured in your environment and in the relationships in which you are involved), your **Result Value** (what you deeply desire as a meaningful outcome for yourself and others), your **Go To Values** (what you leverage with others to move things forward), and your **Accelerator Values** (what you leverage to resource yourself and others in order to get unstuck and move forward again). The process provides a facilitated deep dive not only into what these are but also how they show up and enable potential and purpose. On the opposite page is an example of a values map. For more details, go to www.pursuitinc.com.

There are many models and tools to help individuals reach clarity about their core values and the behaviours needed to support them. Although each of them is slightly different, most follow the same framework: personal reflection, values sort, narrow the field, and personal definition.

Consistent with other exercises I have shared within this book, the values mapping exercises begin with some reflection to help open up your memories and deepen your understanding of what is important to you. The meaningful experience exercise described earlier is a great example of this step. The second step, the values sort, involves reviewing a list of common values—most sets begin with at least fifty—and selecting the fifteen most important to you, ranked as best you can. Each of these exercises also provides space to create a new value or combine several into one that more accurately captures what is important to you. You can find a sample of a values list and my personal values chart at **www.safebravespaces.com**.

Copyright © 2007-2016 Pursuit Development Labs Inc. All Rights Reserved.

Pursuit
Meaningful Pursuits Unleashed

My Values System - Greg Smith

GS Values

Ideal Environment I Create — *Relating with Others* — *How I Initiate*

Go To Value

Driver Value
"What is critical for me to have present & honoured in my environment & the relationships I am involved."

Accelerator Value
"What I leverage to resource myself & others to get unstuck & move forward again."

---

2. Authenticity — **75% Lived**
The journey towards knowing and being fully accepting of self. Self knowledge & acceptance is the cornerstone of personal leadership and creates the space for others to discover the same.

3. Gratitude — **85% Lived**
Striving to live in a state of gratefulness as the starting point to every day. Recognizing and reminding myself of the many blessings that I have in my life opens up personal creativity and abundance thinking

4. Abundance thinking — **80% Lived**
A belief that the world has enough for all. Making daily choices driven by this belief builds bridges, sparks unexpected growth and fulfilment. Discovering that by 'letting go' we makes things grow.

5. Community — **70% Lived**
Recognition that it's not just about us. There is a greater force within positive community. Recognizing, valuing and leveraging others accelerates goals and purpose.

Go To Value
"What I bring & leverage with others to move things forward."

1. Faith/Love — **80% Lived**
Belief that we are here for a purpose, part of a connected work of love. Driven by love as I am loved unconditionally by a higher being.

6. Clarity — **60% Lived**
Our world is overly complicated and filled with 'white noise' which results in misdirection, missed opportunity and hindered impact. Early on clarity on the why, what and how enhances connectedness, personal contribution and fulfilment.

Engaged
When I am aligned in my work, my relationships and things are moving forward, I am engaged & freely leveraging my Go-To Values

Aligned
When my Driver Value is present & honoured in my work and my relationships, and there is an opportunity to achieve my Result Value, I am aligned

Not-Aligned
When my Value Driver is not honoured & is not present or my value result is at risk or won't progress, I am not aligned.

Result Value
"What I deeply desire as a meaningful outcome for myself & others."

Re-Engaged
When things get stuck & stop moving forward easily, I use my Accelerator Values to resource myself to get re-engaged & move things forward.

7. Curiosity — **75% Lived**
Personal growth and advancement within community begins with being curious. Seeking first to understand, especially when an idea or an insight 'rubs you the wrong way'. That is the moment when real growth and big ideas happen

8. Courage — **70% Lived**
Equally important to accelerating any good and meaningful work/results is the willingness to be courageous. Bringing forward 'your truth' in a respectfully direct way stretches both yourself and others in your communities

9. Fulfillment — **80% Lived**
Is experienced as a warm, positive & empowering energy. Occurs when you are 'in flow' with purpose, engaged in relationship (with others or things). Helps activate the 'joy gene' and often accelerates a sense of connectivity and community

10. Joy — **80% Lived**
Joy is holistic state of being when you are overflowing with gratefulness within community (people or nature). When you experience joy it evokes a physical, emotional, mental and spiritual reaction, it creates a pause in the noise, often last only a moment and warms your soul deeply.

Co-creating With Flow — *Direction & Possibilities* — *Creating Breakthroughs*

Ideal Energy I Create — *Relating with Others* — *How I Initiate*

Once you have identified your top fifteen values, most frameworks suggest that you narrow your list down to the top five or ten. I recommend trying to get that number closer to five as it helps you refine what is truly important to you. This is not a simple task: almost everyone I know has found it difficult to narrow the list down. To assist with this step, consider these final five values as core values, which are not optional and not negotiable. These are values that *must exist* in your environments and relationships.

The intention of the fourth step, personal definition, is to enable you to capture and articulate what this value truly means to you and how it is expressed in your everyday life (in other words, you are articulating a virtue). This is a critical step as it allows you to put words to what is important to you. Getting clarity around "what is behind the word" provides tremendous insight to help guide further choices and decisions in your personal journey towards safe brave space. As an example, take a look at my personal value/virtue statements in the personal values map above. The last step in understanding and living your values is a self-evaluation, in which you consider how you "live" the values and see the virtue expressed in your day-to-day life. Norman Schwarzkopf, the retired U.S. Army general and leader of the coalition forces in the Gulf War, famously stated that "the truth of the matter is that you always know the right thing to do. The hardest part is doing it."

Fully living our values is a lifelong work in progress which will have its ebbs and flows. Taking a pulse check along the way allows us to honestly reflect where we are, celebrate where we have made progress and identify one thing that would move us forward. Some helpful questions to guide this pulse check are:

- What percentage of time have I fully lived this value (0%–100%)?
- What are moments of progress (decisions and actions where I have truly lived my values)? How did I feel? What was the impact on me and others?
- What is the one thing I want to do, to even more fully live my values?

Closely linked with your values are the things that you are most passionate about, drawn to, and motivated by. Before you close this step of the knowing process, I would encourage you to consider reflecting on the following actions and capture what themes are bubbling up for you:

1. Review your meaningful experience journal and capture what areas and/or causes that you have found yourself regularly drawn to over your life so far.
2. Look at your book collection, magazines, DVDs, CDs and credit card statements. Notice any themes?
3. What do you love to talk about, learn about and/or teach others about?

Build a Personal Contribution Commitment (PCC) Statement
With a better understanding of the gifts, attributes and strengths that I had to contribute, the way I best worked, and guided by my core values, I was ready to define my unique contribution to the world, often described as a *personal purpose*. The final guidepost answers the questions "why am I here?" and "what do I hope to achieve?" It helps you articulate where and how you want to impact the world. This is often a point at which individuals lose momentum in their self-discovery process, as defining a personal purpose seems too large and unnecessary. Many recent articles have suggested that the word "purpose" itself is too nebulous and often is unrealistic. As a result, I have shifted my language from "personal purpose" to "Personal Contribution Commitment (PCC) statement," as that wording suggests both a guidepost and something that is action-oriented. My PCC has required effort to define and has evolved over time. I believe that spending time reflecting and capturing a PCC statement is the single most important work each of us can do to advance toward the creation of safe brave spaces. A Personal Contribution Commitment statement, thoughtfully crafted, is the booster fuel that releases that inner wisdom and full potential.

Three quick exercises that I have found helpful and often recommend to clients to craft their PCC are (from easiest to more difficult):

1. **Create your billboard.** If you could have a gigantic billboard anywhere with anything on it—metaphorically speaking, getting a message out to millions or billions—what would it say and why? It could be a few words or a paragraph.

2. **Message to a new world.** You are getting into a rocket ship. It takes off. You are on your way to another planet. It's a fine planet in every way, but it's uninhabited. You can shape this planet however you like. You have the power to reshape it any way you want. When you land, what is it that you're going to make happen? What's the impact you want to have that will make the planet the way you want it to be? (Pause). The ship is now landing on the planet. The door opens. You touch the planet and say, "It's going to be this way." What is "this way"?

3. **Questions towards clarity.** Significant questions are often the best way to unveil what you already know to be true but can't yet see. A group called the Positive Project suggests the following exercise to help define your purpose/PCC. Find a quiet place where you won't be disturbed for at least two hours and

   a. Go through and answer each of the questions below;

   b. Once you have answered them all, take time to go back over your answers and find any common themes;

   c. Go back and review all of your answers. Take ten to twenty minutes and think about each of your answers in depth. Ask yourself how you feel when you read your answers. Note which ones move you and which make you feel alive.

   d. Now, write as many answers as you can to the question "My Personal Contribution Commitment statement is ——?" until you feel moved, extreme joy, or are even brought to tears. Once you do this, you will know your PCC.

      • When I was 8 years old, I loved…

      • I lose track of time when I am…

      • If I knew I couldn't fail, I would…

      • I feel great about myself when…

      • If money was not an issue, I would love to spend my time…

- I'm a rock star at…
- Three things I love about myself are…
- If I weren't afraid of what other people think, I would…
- My favourite things to do in my free time are…
- If I knew I was going to die one year from today, I would…
- Two people who inspire me most are…
- I would regret not doing these things in my life…

Here are two examples to help get you started and to provide some inspiration:

- Greg's PCC statement: *"Creating and enabling safe brave spaces, where hearts are evoked, confidence is enhanced, and potential is realized."*
- Greg's Sample #2: *"Empowering others to be more effective leaders and fulfilled people through authentic and thoughtful connection. I am committed to realizing dreams—for both myself and those who cross my path. Above all else, I am committed to leading a life of love, thoughtfulness, and happiness."*

My Unique Approach

Once you have uncovered your strengths and gifts (what you bring), your values and passions (what you care about), and your personal contribution commitment (where and how you want to impact), it is also important to capture your unique approach (how you work best). This will be unearthed within your meaningful moments and gifts discovery exercises, and can be further revealed by personal assessments. My three favourite assessments, two of which I have already mentioned, are Kolbe, the enneagram (EQi19) and the EQi 2.0 emotional intelligence index. Each of these helps flesh out our unique and best way of working and connecting with others. Personally, I have leveraged the support of a coach to help understand and apply insights from these tools. This work lets us fully access our unique approaches, enabling us to maximize our energy, potential and impact.

Blockers, Triggers and Truths

An outcome of defining my gifts, values and purpose is a growing sense of confidence and clarity about what is important to me. The more that confidence grows, the more I am influenced by what I will call "my truth." The reality of the world and the benefit of community is that there is actually a "broader truth" that, when understood, helps release my potential and that of those around me. To be more open to that broader truth, I needed to pause and reflect before moving forward on the things that might inhibit that openness—the dark side of the story, my fears and biases. The fact that this was not a place I had spent too much time was quickly made clear by the lack of Post-its on my ME Wall under this category. Most people would describe me as a "cup-half-full" person who is optimistic, sees only the positives and as a result can sometimes dismiss those who live more fully in what some might call "reality." My wife Josette is one of those individuals and although I am grateful that she provides my balance in each situation, I am certain she would say that I sometimes avoid and/or dismiss the hard reality in front of me.

In tackling this exploration of fears and biases, as with the work on gifts, values and purpose, I began by leveraging some excellent tools that already existed, journaling my experiences and identifying themes and opportunities to grow. I began to understand that, like energy, fears and biases are not good or bad but, rather, reactions and responses to the energy disruptions in one's life. Stuff happens and we learn through experience and sometimes innate strengths to respond. Greater awareness of the patterns that have been formed over our lives, combined with our enhanced ability to pause, allows us to recognize the triggers, tap into our whole selves—the reservoir we talked about earlier—and choose how we wish to respond. We will dive deeper into some simple approaches to do this in the sections on Letting Go and Showing Up, but the first job is to better understand the unique fears and biases within ourselves.

Fears

As shared earlier, I am not naturally moved to spend time uncovering things that make either me or others uncomfortable. Throughout my life I have been seen as an optimistic person who can be counted on to see the silver lining. I recognize now that I had developed a pattern of avoiding the full truth of many situations and preferred to simply shift myself and others to a better situation rather than sit a bit and learn from the present. Although this gift of being optimistic can be helpful in many situations and has resulted in a reputation for being inspirational and even visionary, it can also create an environment marked by confusion, frustration and lack of realism. An additional problem for me was that a reputation as a "nice guy" often resulted in others not wanting to provide me honest feedback about this blind spot. Fortunately, one friend had the courage to suggest that I might want to consider leveraging a tool called the enneagram to help provide a broader picture of the fears and motivations that were influencing my actions.

Although I am certified in many tools, I had never heard of the enneagram. I was surprised to learn that the core model had remained relatively unchanged for over 3,000 years. This, combined with the fact that it also contained a mathematical formula and that I could find it throughout the world in many traditions, further inflamed my imagination and interest. I will admit that I am a self-proclaimed assessment geek, driven by my belief in the importance of enhancing self-awareness for both personal and leadership growth. As most assessment tools are *self*-assessments, I don't believe they are the answer to everything, and I don't believe that we should use them to put people in boxes. Unfortunately, the use of various tools without proper coaching and facilitation results in labelling, not learning. If we view assessments as tools to open our thinking and to spark personal exploration through dialogue, then we truly tap into their benefits. Within that context, I found the enneagram to be most thorough and impactful, and since introducing it within my coaching practice almost every client has expressed the same view.

The enneagram is unique because it is less about "putting people in a box" and more about identifying where you are today, how being you has made you successful, and helping you see strengths that could be leveraged more as well as areas that might be developed further. It helps uncover the core fears and needs that release your unique way of responding and provides insights into how your innate response can help and hinder. Understanding these insights, the patterns that I had built up over the years, and some alternate pathways to response provided an important missing piece in my "ME Search." For me personally, as a Type 7, I discovered that a core need to feel safe had resulted in a fear of being limited and an aversion to anything that seemed painful. This revelation resonated with me and helped me to be more open to exploring past behaviours and how they enhanced or inhibited the creation of safe brave spaces within myself and others. In the next chapter, ME Growing, I will highlight the importance of sharing your insights and the benefit of finding a coach to help deepen understanding and speed up growth. For more information about the enneagram itself, check out **www.safebravespaces.com**.

Unconscious/Implicit Biases

The second area of awareness I needed to investigate was unconscious or implicit biases. Studies show we all are biased, and we don't even know it. As humans, thousands of messages bombard our brains each second. Instead of constantly seeing the world as if for the very first time, our brains have learned to work more efficiently by following this pathway:

1. **Our experience.** Our minds archive patterns and associations we observe throughout our upbringing, from family, education, peer groups, media exposure and other life experiences.
2. **Our decisions.** We have evolved to process 200,000 times more information by making rapid unconscious decisions based on assumptions we make from our archive of patterns and associations
3. **Our unconscious bias.** The result is that we are no longer neutral. If we have seen two "things" occur together, our unconscious mind assumes we'll see them together again. As a result, we display micro-behaviours and unknowingly discriminate against one group and in favour of another.

There are at least twenty cognitive biases that interrupt our decision-making process. Three of the most common are (1) *affinity bias*, where we ignore negative traits of people we like and focus on the faults of those we don't; (2) *confirmation bias*, where we seek facts that will confirm our existing pre-conceptions; and (3) *social comparison bias*, where we don't compete with certain strengths of others.

Realizing the reality of unconscious biases is an important step as it helps us recognize triggers for them and put in place checkpoints to monitor and manage these unconscious assumptions. There are several excellent tools available to help mine these biases, including Project Implicit. This initiative, created by Harvard University researchers, assesses "conscious and unconscious preferences for over 90 different topics." It's a great place to start, it only takes around fifteen minutes, and you may be very surprised by the results.

Uncovering my fears and biases was a critical component of my ME Search and helped equip me to build a workout plan to enhance my safe brave muscles. There was, however, one last area that I felt I needed to explore, one that I know is a difficult subject for many and one I had not stopped to deeply consider prior to this. We know this place as "privilege."

Privilege and Blind Spots

Over the past ten years I have become more aware of how privileged I am as an older white male, raised in a loving middle-class, white-collar family in Canada. I consider myself to be a fairly progressive thinker, grateful for my circumstances and continually evolving through the coaching of my spouse and children. Throughout most of my career I have had the opportunity, while holding senior leadership positions, to help create "safe brave spaces" in which team members individually and collectively discovered and appreciated their unique strengths, approaches and purpose. During these opportunities I have also experienced growth and awakening to my biases, my fears and my privilege and how they sometimes hinder my awareness of both what I see and how I respond.

A few months ago, after watching a tweet from James Corden of Alexandria Ocasio-Cortez asking powerful questions of the House Oversight Committee, I made the comment to my wife and daughter how much I appreciated how she calmly, respectfully and yet forcefully challenged the status quo to start to change. I then commented that I believed that this approach "was so much better than when people scream in anger."

One hour after that conversation I was in our kitchen, loading the dishwasher, when my daughter entered and in a calm voice said, "Dad, do you have a minute?" I have learned that this statement from my wise 29-year-old usually portends an E.F. Hutton moment for me (if you are under the age of 40 you will have to Google their old ads to understand what I mean). Her statement and follow-up question modelled the best of what I have learned and have tried to espouse to enable safe brave spaces. She began with an observation: "Dad, I've noticed that sometimes when commenting on the approaches of those from whom you may have a different perspective, you speak in a negative tone that may devalue both the person and their perspective. For me, it is especially difficult when it is something that I believe in."

I wish that I could say that I responded with wisdom and curiosity, but as with most things for me, I still needed time to unconsciously and consciously reflect. Instead, in the moment, I quickly shifted to fear and justification, not honouring her courage but choosing to "help her see my perspective" and defend my viewpoint. Throughout the conversation, although I began to see that my view was clearly from a privileged perspective, I was so caught up in my need to be heard and to be right that I did not "seek to understand" but "forced my understanding," resulting in a posture of judgement which minimized the safe brave spaces that I espouse. We ended our conversation cordially, hugged and called it a night.

This one courageous, curious question from my daughter then began its work. At 5 a.m. I awoke from several dreams with an awareness of how far I still needed to grow in this space to more consistently live my values of being aware, awakened, curious and courageous.

Some tools and frameworks already mentioned in the book, such as ELOPE and SNAP, are helping me to become more aware of what is happening around me, including taking into account the emotions and perspectives of others, especially those I disagree with. One of the most helpful books that has deepened my awareness in this area is *So You Want to Talk About Race* by Ijeoma Oluo. She provides one of the best definitions of privilege and also a brilliant suggestion: to regularly conduct an "advantage check," which is simply a listing of the areas in which you have an advantage over others. She states that she does this annually herself, and when I did one, I recognized several items beyond those mentioned at the beginning of the book. I had missed many things, including that the fact that (1) I am a Canadian citizen; (2) I am able-bodied; and (3) I had access to a benefits program to cover all my health and dental needs.

Being more awakened to the biases and privileges that influence how I see, what I hear and how I feel helps me to be more curious about understanding what's behind what another person is saying or feeling before I choose to contribute to the conversation myself. This more elevated state allows me to be courageous and to challenge my thinking, to recognize my privilege, to be vulnerable, to truly participate rather than propagate. For additional tools to help enhance self-awareness around privilege and blind spots go to **www.safebravespaces.com**.

Take some time to reflect and consider the things you have just read in this critical first step in your ME Search. The following questions will help you begin the journey and test out some tools and/or frameworks that resonate most in this moment.

What resonated most as "true" for you within this section? Why? What most challenges and/or churns within you? Why?

- On a scale of 1 to 10 (10 being "very well"), how well do you "know" your *Strengths/Gifts* (aka *What you Bring*); *Values and Passions* (aka *What You Care About*); *Unique Approach* (aka *How You Work Best*); *Fears & Biases* (aka *What Gets in Your Way*); and/ or *Personal Contribution Commitment* (*Where and How You Want to Impact*)?
- Which area would be most valuable to explore and expand further?
- Select one exercise to strengthen your selected area of focus.
- What insights are you learning from this exercise?

Pulling It All Together:
Creating Your "Being ME" Profile and a Safe Brave Plan

As I completed the Knowing phase of understanding ME, I quickly realized that I had unearthed a lot of information. My ME Wall helped me narrow down the critical themes and insights. To make this actionable, I needed to create a simple one-page summary for easy reference. This summary has over the years evolved into what I call my "Being ME" Profile and my "Safe Brave Plan." This double-sided, one-sheet document has become a valuable tool to keep me focused, to share with others, and to help me reflect as I strengthen the safe brave space within myself. You'll find these documents on the next two pages.

Before leaving the Knowing phase I would encourage you to review all of your work and begin populating your Being ME Profile and Safe Brave Plan. This is your first draft; it will evolve over time and will become a touchstone to help guide your entire safe brave spaces journey. You can find templates for the Being ME Profile and Safe Brave Plan on the SBS website.

Leveraging my Being Me Profile together with my Safe Brave Me plan, I continue to evolve, sometimes very slowly. My goal is to move my "mirror of self-awareness" out in front of my eyes so I catch myself before I act. Through this first step of knowing, I have deepened my understanding of ME, and have come a long way from in the beginning having no mirror at all. Now I have moved the mirror to my side, thus seeing many things as they are happening—yet often still too late. My hope in writing this book is to encourage us all to find our mirrors, to become more aware, awakened, curious and courageous, through which we will enable the safe brave spaces within our relationships and the communities within which we live and work. This leads me to the second phase of ME: Growing.

My Being ME Profile

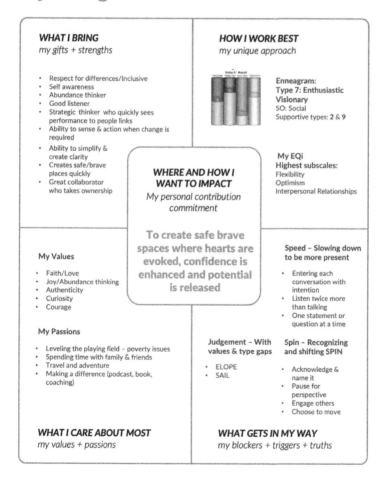

WHAT I BRING
my gifts + strengths

- Respect for differences/Inclusive
- Self awareness
- Abundance thinker
- Good listener
- Strategic thinker who quickly sees performance to people links
- Ability to sense & action when change is required
- Ability to simplify & create clarity
- Creates safe/brave places quickly
- Great collaborator who takes ownership

HOW I WORK BEST
my unique approach

Enneagram:
Type 7: Enthusiastic
Visionary
SO: Social
Supportive types: 2 & 9

My EQi
Highest subscales:
Flexibility
Optimism
Interpersonal Relationships

WHERE AND HOW I WANT TO IMPACT
My personal contribution commitment

To create safe brave spaces where hearts are evoked, confidence is enhanced and potential is released

My Values

- Faith/Love
- Joy/Abundance thinking
- Authenticity
- Curiosity
- Courage

Speed – Slowing down to be more present

- Entering each conversation with intention
- Listen twice more than talking
- One statement or question at a time

My Passions

- Leveling the playing field – poverty issues
- Spending time with family & friends
- Travel and adventure
- Making a difference (podcast, book, coaching)

Judgement – With values & type gaps

- ELOPE
- SAIL

Spin – Recognizing and shifting SPIN

- Acknowledge & name it
- Pause for perspective
- Engage others
- Choose to move

WHAT I CARE ABOUT MOST
my values + passions

WHAT GETS IN MY WAY
my blockers + triggers + truths

My Safe Brave ME Map

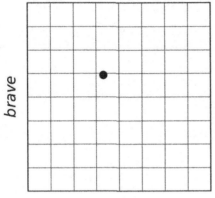

brave

safe

being brave
doing, actioning, releasing the unencumbered freedom to stand for what you believe in and supporting others to do the same

being safe
understanding, accepting, and trusting yourself and supporting others to do the same

My Safe Brave ME Plan

Being Safe Goal The one thing that will most enhance your Safe	**What actions will I take to achieve it?**	**What success looks like?**	**Who can help?**
Create personal safe brave circle to support growth & enhance safe brave spaces • Phil D, Steve G, Jan O, Jacki, Peter S	• Call each & share my vision • Build simple framework to guide dialogue • Schedule first meeting	• Deepened relationship with group • Support in each others' journeys	• Jacki as co-partner
Being Brave Goal The one thing that will most enhance your Brave	**What actions will I take to achieve it?**	**What success looks like?**	**Who can help?**
More boldly share my truth by listening to and actioning my instincts	• Be more real with Josette by acknowledging emotions and sharing disconnects • Positively challenge and share contrary thoughts bubbling up instinctually	• Deepened relationship, Josette and I are even more respectfully, lovingly direct • Inner circle, trusted community comment on increased voice & courage	• Josette – engage in plan • Witness/accountability partner o L9 o Danica

growing

Growing ME

Growing is about investing in, accepting, loving, trusting and expanding this understanding of ME and identifying one or two focus areas for growth as the foundation for your personal safe brave plan. The Knowing phase allowed me to gain a clear perspective on what I believed about myself, what I valued, and how best I could contribute to the world. It created a safe place for me to re-discover an awareness of self and helped inform my safe brave plan. With a clear picture of ME, the second phase was to socialize my understanding of ME within my inner circle. My inner circle is tight and includes a small number of people with whom I can share openly and where I feel open to receive feedback. As already noted, throughout my life I have believed that "everything happens in-between." All of my experiences, my values and even my personal contribution commitment have been shaped by those around me. I believe that we create a unique perspective, our path is our own, and it is influenced by our response and reaction to the input and experiences that we have received. At the beginning of the book, I talked about the importance of energy, its impact on and importance for our journey, and the fact that one of the biggest sources of energy is those that we interact with. It is one thing to know this, another to proactively choose to tap into that energy to reveal a broader view of ourselves and to be open to the insights and ideas of those around us. This is the first step in moving from Knowing to Growing. It allows you to deepen your self-awareness beyond your line of sight and begin to broaden your truth about yourself. This step requires us to be brave.

Choosing your inner circle will depend on your level of confidence. Sharing, no matter how prepared you are, creates a vulnerability many of us aren't comfortable with. I have always considered myself a transparent, authentic individual who was self-aware and open to share. My self-discovery process revealed many hidden truths about me I felt I had kept well-hidden for most of my life. The reality was that I wasn't as good an actor as I thought I was, and those closest to me already knew and were very open to supporting the full release of my bigger self. Even with a fairly high level of confidence I began my external exploration with a small group of people, including my wife, my kids, and two close friends, with both of whom I had already experienced shared significant challenges. In each case, these people had seen me at what I considered my best and worst and I knew that they would be honest, encouraging, and would provide a perspective that would deepen my understanding of ME. My process of deepening the understanding of ME was simple and followed a consistent framework:

1. Share my intention—what I was doing, why I was doing it, and why it was important to me.
2. Set and accept the request—be clear about what I wanted from them (i.e., honest and direct feedback, observations and examples that contribute to and build upon my ME search, and their agreement to take part).
3. Share, listen, inquire, explore.
4. Express gratitude and enroll them as supporters.

This first phase in Growing strengthened both my safe and brave muscles and increased my confidence and courage to widen the circle into my trusted community. My trusted community is the next layer of family and friends who know me, had historically supported me, and who had previously showed what others have called "radical candor," that is, respectfully direct feedback. Adam Grant suggests that to maximize the opportunity for growth, it is helpful to include folks whose conclusions you may disagree with but whose thought processes impress or intrigue you. For me, this included my siblings, six personal friends, two former bosses, five former and current peers, and four former team members who reported to me. As many of these folks were living in close proximity, I captured their feedback through phone calls, video calls and in-person coffees (pre-pandemic) using a consistent framework that leveraged many of the key questions from the "Best Self Exercise" developed by the University of Michigan. For these dialogues I used the following simplified framework:

1. I shared my intention—what I was doing, why I was doing it, and why it was important to me.
2. I asked the following question: What would you describe as my greatest strengths, including specific examples of ways in which I used these strengths meaningfully to you?
3. I shared my "Being ME" profile.
4. I asked the following questions:
a. What do you see as blind spots in me that have gotten and may again get in my way in achieving my personal contribution commitment?
b. What do you want me to know and believe about myself that I just don't see?
c. What is the one thing that would have the greatest impact on my journey towards "playing big" and living my purpose?
5. I listened, inquired, explored and captured their insights.
6. I expressed gratitude for their honesty.

Following these meetings, take time (as I did) to reflect on the input they have given you. Identify any additional insights that resonate as "true for you" and update your "Being ME" profile and safe brave plan. With this completed, I felt a deeper understanding of ME and felt more confident and prepared to "Show Up" more consistently and fully as my true and whole self. I also quickly realized that before I "Showed Up" I needed to learn how to "Let Go."

Community is critical to advancing growth and enabling momentum as you start on your safe brave spaces journey. Consider taking a quick pause to reflect on how and with whom to deepen your "ME Search." The following questions will help you begin the journey and test out some tools and/or frameworks that resonate most in this moment.

- What resonated most as "true" for you within you this section? Why? What most challenges and/or churns within you? Why?
- What one or two early ideas do you need to incorporate into your safe brave plan?
- Who would you consider as your "inner circle"?
- Who would you consider being within your "trusted community"?
- Select one exercise or tool to help deepen your ME awareness.
- Reflect on and capture any insights you learned from this exercise.
- Update your Being ME profile with any insights from your inner circle and trusted community.

Letting Go of What Hinders ME

"Let go of who you think you're supposed to be;
embrace who you are."
—Brené Brown

● **letting go**

Critics, Triggers and Truth

As I shared earlier, Letting Go and Showing Up are critical to strengthening our brave muscles and opening up brave spaces as they spark curiosity, courage, openness and connectivity. Letting Go is about forgiveness, forgetting and freeing us from the patterns and responses that inhibit us. With a clearer understanding of myself through the Knowing and Growing phases, I experienced a growth in my ability to feel safe and be confident in who I was, how I wanted to be and where I could impact. As I completed the Knowing and Growing phase, I felt the wind was at my back, momentum was building, and just as I was about to take that leap of faith, a familiar group of "frienemies" came to visit. For me their names are self-doubt, worry, what-if, and shoulda.

I am always surprised by these surprise visits as I am normally a positive, enthusiastic and confident person. I know that they most often show up when I run into something that's important in my system of values and about which my perspective may differ from those of people around me. Or sometimes they make themselves felt in situations where I know I need to stretch. My natural style loves creating a spirit of connecting and community, something which occasionally restrains me from being my full self. If I don't fully show up, then self-doubt is unlikely to visit. But in moments when I pushed through, my "freinemies" were always the first at the door.

Let me give you a simple example of this. We were visiting some good friends and their son was showing me a new hoverboard he had received for his birthday. This ten-year-old and his seven-year-old brother were zipping around the house with ease, and it looked like a lot of fun. I had never done this before, and my adventurous spirit led me to volunteer to try. Following my first fall, the frienemies arrived…. *What are you doing, Greg? You look like a fool! You will never be able to do this!* A mind storm sparked by my frienemies was in full force, further disrupting my confidence and balance. After the fourth fall, the energy insight from my Toys "R" Us experience hit me, and within minutes I was out of my head and into my flow, which resulted in me sailing smoothly (OK, still a bit shaky) around the house on the hoverboard. On my drive home from the party, I mused over what had enabled this quick shift from critic to trigger and truth.

Three months later, as I was gaining momentum on this book, my frienemies showed up again, this time beginning in a dream. In the dream I was Superman. My wife always laughs that most of my dreams are very fantastical, exciting and, even if challenging, are still resolved positively before I wake up. But this dream was different. Although I was Superman, I was struggling. I knew this wasn't my normal type of dream as it began with me in a drugstore washroom struggling to get my "onesie" off. This seemed strange, as I couldn't imagine Superman needing to go to the washroom. In the next scene of my dream, I was trying to fly to a place where I was needed, but it was as if my powers of flight were malfunctioning and I was having trouble staying airborne. I became frustrated and distracted trying to figure out what was wrong. As I sputtered down the street, I shifted from frustration to anger when a transport truck almost ran me over because I was moving so slowly. I felt embarrassed, defeated and inadequate. This is exactly how I normally feel when I allow self-doubt to take hold of my mind.

Whether it is a dream or daydream, I am struck by the fact that each of us are amazing writers, directors and producers of our own movies. The speed and quality of the films we create, often starring the principal characters of anxiety and self-doubt, are amazing. Not only are we the creators of these masterpieces, we also then easily transition to "critic," further adding to our anxiety and self-doubt. This results in what I've called a mind storm, a tornado of negative thoughts so powerful that it can tear apart core elements of who I am and what I uniquely bring to the world.

Any great script begins with a personal experience that the screenwriter has either experienced or researched. With this experience as the core idea, they flesh out the history leading up to the event and the characters taking part in the story. As a screenplay evolves, more writers may join in to help build upon the idea and broaden the viewpoint by providing input from their individual perspectives. Ideas are debated, shaped and tweaked until the story is ready for production. Sometimes the story is so big that there are opportunities for a series or a franchise of stories that extend the experience beyond the moment, enabling the viewer to see the fuller journey of the characters and the ideas they are inspiring.

I believe that our personal scripts are very similar, in that they are usually created over time and influenced by those around us. Most writers will tell you they have multiple stories playing out in their heads and in their journals at the same time. This is certainly true in my life and in my mind. Each moment, every experience that I have is captured in my mind's "journal" and, through the workings of the incredible database that is our brain, connected to the core beliefs and biases that I have been assembling since I was very young. Earlier I shared that while I was writing this book my brother-in-law—who is also a playwright, author and actor—suggested that I consider creating a story wall by using Post-its to capture all of my ideas. He recommended that I remain fluid in my placement of the Post-its and over time simply allow the wall to come together. I have discovered that my mind acts in the same way as my wall; I am learning to allow the story to evolve rather than "lock in the script."

Something unique about our personal stories is that the writer/director—each of us—can re-write and adjust the story as it evolves in real time. Normally in these situations the core elements and themes of the story stay the same and yet there is a fluidity that brings with it excitement and engagement. When we hold on to our core story and frameworks but otherwise allow ourselves to let go, observing, reflecting and even re-writing our scripts, our best work is unveiled. Recognizing and acting on these opportunities for rewrites releases our brave enabling greater voice, contribution and impact.

While we're writing our stories, unfortunately our self-critics sometimes show up and hinder us. They also attack our ability to feel safe. Continuing with the analogy of the screenwriter, once the latest episode is released, it is very hard to stop the critics from arriving. It's like having my very own personalized Rotten Tomatoes website constantly running though my head, led by the most famous and trusted critic of all: me. The thing about critics, especially the inner critic, is that they are neither good nor bad. The key is to accept they exist, learn to decipher what they're saying, and decide if there is anything valuable for you to consider as you write the next script.

The morning after my Superman dream, the clouds in my mind were building—not yet a full storm, but the wind was picking up and visibility was severely reduced. The blustery words of the critics were coming from every direction within the storm: "What right does he have to write a book!" "His insights aren't useful." "What a waste of time and money that book would be!" I felt myself slipping into a tailspin with negative energy surging.

I will share some insights that have helped me let go of these doubts and critics. But first you need to *find them, name them,* and *know when they show up.* Here's a quick framework that has helped me mine this data and use it to advance my "ME Search":

- **Track** the critic visits.
  - o **Sense** it: Activate your Doppler radar to detect negative energy spikes.
  - o **Name** the emotion associated with the energy.
  - o **Record** it: Capture...
    - The critic's message (don't engage with it; just write it down).
    - The situation when the message arrived (where you were, what you were doing, who was there).
    - Your response (either actual or initial intention).
    - The outcome of your response.
- **Create** the critic profile:
  - o The critic's name.
  - o Their most common messages.
  - o When they most regularly show up.

This framework has helped me to build awareness of my critics and to better respond when they do decide to show up. I normally revisit this process at least once a year, as I have discovered the cast of critics can shift over time.

Managing My Critics

Earlier in the book I shared that learning the power to pause had helped me shift my perspectives in times of energy surges. Pausing has also proven very helpful in dealing with a low rumbling of energy created by self-doubt initiated by my self-critics. This energy is often subtle in how it manifests itself. You know it is there, but it seems to be hidden and therefore not obvious. Yet it can build quickly. The pause forces you to clear your mind of thoughts that cloud your deeper awareness of what is happening. To respond to the critics, both loud and subtle, you first need to pause. I have discovered through my meditation work that an important enabler of our ability to pause is breathing and connecting to our senses. Aside from the exercises I shared earlier, I have discovered the following three simple ways to access my breath, my senses and disrupt my critics:

- Three Breaths > Take three deep breaths while saying "breathing in" and "breathing out"; or try
- 5–4–3–2–1 > A simple settling technique that ties to your senses. When anxiety sets in...
  - With your eyes identify 5 things.
  - With your ears identify 4 sounds.
  - With your nose identify 3 smells.
  - With your hands feel 2 textures.
  - With your mouth identify 1 taste.
- Use the "Happy Birthday" tune > This last technique is particularly effective in "pausing" the critic. Take the doubts into your head and sing them to the tune of "Happy birthday." It is amazing how this one simple step forces you to laugh and temporarily disconnect from the doubts.

The morning following my Superman dream, coffee in hand, I moved to my regular quiet spot, took three breaths, and began my normal practice of reading an inspirational quotation or verse. I normally combine this with a prayer or conversation with God to reflect on what I have read. For you it may be a reflection on the beauty of nature, a letting go to the universe or an inward reflection.

This first step always allows me to connect with someone or something bigger than myself. There is something about this realization that calms the mind storm. Curiously enough, the morning of this storm, my reflection was of King David trapped in a cave hiding from his enemies, totally broken as he had run out of options and ideas. He too was experiencing a significant mind storm, seeing the tornado on the horizon with no place to hide.

As I reflected and conversed with what I call God, I heard the words "Let Go." Even now, as I write these words, I remember the shiver that went through my body and the sense of release. It was as if suddenly there was a slight break in the clouds and a tiny ray of sunshine broke through. I wasn't yet clear about what this meant; however, I knew I had made a shift. In this shifted moment, Letting Go meant choosing to ELOPE, the technique I shared earlier. The pause allowed me to recognize and accept that what I was feeling was energy, which I have the ability to channel. This acknowledgment shifted me from my head to my heart, and to a state of love and gratefulness for both the potential use of this energy and my growing ability to learn to pause. This heightened sense of appreciation opened me to discovering what was really true and what I might learn in this moment. This openness allowed me to become more present to what was happening and engage with my deeper wisdom, experiences and instincts to uncover the truer reality of my situation.

When I reach this place of deeper wisdom, I can recognize more clearly the triggers and see the critics that have created my doubts, and then go on to discover the actual truth of the situation. With this clarity, I can better discern the situation and also make better decisions. When I can get to this place, I am more fully releasing both my safe and brave muscles. When my critics arrive out of the blue, I need to quickly shift from triggers to truth. After I ELOPE, I then—

1. Turn down the volume (visualize turning down the volume on the critic) and
2. Learn to SAIL. When you are triggered and sense your energy and emotions building …
   o S—Stop and breathe.
   o A—Acknowledge and allow (remember, energy/emotion is not you; it is simply happening to you).
   o I—Investigate. > What might be behind this? How does it impact you and others when you feel this way? Is this helpful?
   o L—Learn and Let Go. >Observe it, don't identify with it. Ask yourself: Is this something I can learn from and then let it go? ("Use. then lose.")

Here is how I leveraged SAIL the morning that my critic showed up:

• S—As I sat within my place of deeper awareness, I **stopped** and focused on my breath. Like a great stretching exercise, with every breath I went even deeper and become more peaceful.

- A—In this deeper place of awareness and peace I simply **acknowledged** and allowed the situation, this critic's claims that I had "no right to write a book," my ideas were "too insignificant," etc. I could name the accompanying emotions that I felt when I heard those voices and recognize them as just reactions.
- I—Leveraging this fuller wisdom and peace, I could more objectively **investigate** this critical review, bringing in all the facts and experiences it referred to.
- L—With this broader view I could then decide whether there was anything to **learn** and after that simply **let go**. In this case, I saw that the actual truth was that I had over 35 years of significant experience, had been encouraged by others to capture my insights, and knew from recent speeches I had given that the ideas resonated as true not just for me but to others, too.

Richika Jain suggests that "worries and tension are like birds. We cannot stop them from flying near us. But we certainly can stop them from making a nest in our mind." By more consistently applying some of the above exercises, I have been more successful in keeping those nests from being built and moving from critic to triggers to truth, rechannelling the negative energy towards positive action and expanded safe and brave spaces within myself.

One final insight. Besides my critics, the other things I need to learn to let go of are attributes that sometimes result in the overuse of my strengths. One example is my innate ability to think quickly and logically, to connect the dots before others in the room. Sometimes when I overuse this gift, it results in me being stuck in a thinking loop that is often the spark that ignites the energy storms.

Choosing to ELOPE and SAIL when this happens has proven equally helpful in quickly bringing me back to a place of deeper wisdom that leads to the better discernment and decisions critical to Showing Up. You'll find additional resources to help Let Go on the SBS site.

Letting Go, especially Letting Go of deeply ingrained behaviour that may be unconscious, is a difficult and highly rewarding step in the journey. The following questions will help you begin the journey and test out some tools and/or frameworks to help you release the things that are hindering your growth in this moment.

- What resonated most as "true" for you within this section? Why? What most challenges and/or churns within you? Why?
- Review any previous work around fears, biases or privilege.
- Reflect on this work: What surprised you? What convicted you? What most hinders you personally from being more fully safe and brave?
- Select on exercise or tool to begin letting go of that hindrance.
- Reflect on and capture any insights you gained from this exercise.
- Update your Being ME profile and Safe Brave Plan with any insights.

Showing Up as Fully ME

• showing up

Equipped with my newly found knowledge of ME, including the importance of Letting Go, the last step within the "Starting within Me" process is establishing some habits to support fully Showing Up. This is all about putting what I have discovered into practice and beginning to act upon the idea of safe brave spaces, starting with me. I have discovered through many failed new year's resolution lists that to live your commitments you need a solid plan. "Starting within ME" is driven by the insights that others need to see to believe. In order for me to enable safe brave spaces, I needed to show them within myself every day. When in the past I have been successful with a shift in my life, I know that it required me to Start Strong, Stretch Often and Reflect, Recharge and Revise.

This idea of the need to Start Strong, Stretch Often and Reflect, Recharge and Revise is exemplified by high-performance athletes. As a young kid growing up in Brantford, Ontario, I could see this firsthand with a schoolmate who would become the greatest hockey player in the world. When I was in elementary school, a group of us asked Wayne if he wanted to go to the movies with us. He said no, he wanted to spend more time practicing. As twelve-year-olds, we thought, "What a loser!" In a few years this thought changed to "Why didn't *I* practice?" Although the specifics of this story have been blurred by the years, I recognize now that Wayne's commitment to starting strong, stretching often, and reflecting/recharging and revising his techniques all helped him refine his amazing gifts to fully enable the greatness that he was to embody.

Earlier I mentioned the book *The Power of Full Engagement: Managing Energy, Not Time* by Jim Loehr and Tony Schwartz. Although they are most known for their work in the corporate world, they began their work with high-performance athletes and recognized the same truths in that work.

Starting Strong

Within the sphere of sports, I have always appreciated the grace and power of short-distance runners. Living in Oakville, Ontario, I deepened that connection by emotionally taking part with Donovan Bailey when he won the gold medal in the 100 metres at the 1996 Olympics. Any sprinter will confirm that a key to success is having a quick, smooth start. Practicing your ability to get out of the gate quickly will significantly increase your likelihood of success. Similarly, building a daily habit to initiate my Showing Up has been critical. The daily devotion, meditation and stretching that I described earlier are the perfect ingredients to enable readiness for the day. Creating a morning habit of rising early and committing to the moment of pause allows me to put things into perspective. This daily pause allows me to narrow my focus to this moment and this day and build a simple plan of how I wish to show up for the next 24 hours. This is a more manageable amount of time and I am struck by the power of this simple act of focus. From this state of pause and focus, I reground myself in two realities.

The first reality is that I have the full ability to choose my response. In many circumstances, I cannot choose what happens to me; however, as I fully tap into my deeper self-awareness, I have 100 percent ability to choose my response. The more I choose to ELOPE and SAIL, the better those choices become. The second reality is that I can decide where and how I should respond by recognizing and accepting the difference between concern, influence and control. Stephen Covey captured this brilliantly in his book *The Seven Habits of Highly Effective People*. He suggests that while there are many things that we may be concerned about, we should ask ourselves "What do we have control over?" and "Where might we have the ability to influence?"

This second reality is freeing as it provides us the opportunity to focus on the things we can either influence and/or control, allowing more time to release our potential. It is so easy to get lost in and overwhelmed by the things we are concerned about in the world and cannot impact. Beginning with the core of what you control and stretching into where you can influence will create the momentum that we spoke about earlier in the book.

Beginning with a commitment to starting strong and supported by these two realities, we are better prepared and will more consistently have a quick, smooth start towards fully Showing Up. These insights comprise a simple model that I have added at the end of my devotion, meditation and stretching, a little TLC or 3-2-1.

- **Talents**—Three things that I bring. Reminding ourselves of three unique gifts, experiences and/or perspectives reinforces our confidence and helps us to tap into the beauty of our ME Search. This daily simple reminder deepens personal safe space and stokes the fire of our "brave."
- **Love**—Two things I am grateful for. Gratitude is a well-researched

topic; it's the booster fuel for activating your contribution to the world. It is also the foundation for openness and curiosity, which lead to further growth in this development cycle.

- **Contribution**—One specific action. One of my favourite books over the past few years has been *The One Thing* by Gary Keller and Jay Papasan. What I so appreciate about it is its simplicity and focus. As someone full of ideas who sometimes over-commits, I found that adapting the book's core insight to identify the one thing that, upon doing it, would most enhance safe brave space for myself and for others each day has significantly increased my level of personal impact. To add to the likelihood of impact, I use a bit of visualization simply by—
  o Closing my eyes and thinking of one person whose space I can make safer and/or braver today. It may be me; it may be someone at home or someone at work.
  o Thinking of one thing I can do to advance the safe brave space of that person. I find it helpful to visualize myself doing this.
  o Last step.... Opening my eyes and putting this connection/ action in my calendar or "next action" list.

Stretching Often

Having a strong start is key and, like world-class athletes, we must recognize the need to keep limber throughout the day. The second step of Showing Up is to find ways to "Stretch Often" during your day, continuing to work your safe and brave muscles in every moment. Two exercises that have helped me are:

- Mini mindset muscle builders > Tapping into the power of personal control before I enter into any situation, I try to ask myself two questions (depending on how much control you have over your calendar, blocking out five minutes before any meeting will help strengthen this practice):
  o To release my fullest potential and contribution, do I need to flex more safe or more brave?
  o What does more safe or more brave look like in this moment?

- Safe Brave Tracker > Many of the apps on my iPhone have tracking features that allow me to record my progress. Recognizing the importance of strengthening both my safe and brave muscles, I have a simple reminder that pops up at 12 noon and 5 p.m. and prompts me to "Pause and capture personal safe and brave advancements." It's important both to capture what happened and the impact on yourself and others.

One last insight around the importance of stretching involves energy. Foundational to maintaining and growing levels of safe and brave is your energy in all four areas: physical, emotional, mental and spiritual. Building intentional and regular activities to strengthen each area will increase your ability to enhance your personal safe brave spaces.

Reflect, Recharge and Revise

Every athlete recognizes that to increase how consistently they Show Up at their best, they need moments to reflect, recharge and revise. A recent coaching program I took part in provided a straightforward framework that helped evolve what I call my Safe Brave Spaces Reflection Calendar.

You should consider each of the time frames set out below to be sacred, unmovable except for extreme emergencies, and blocked off in your calendar. Before I enter each of the reflection moments described below, I first re-ground myself on my safe brave plan by reviewing my ME Profile, focusing especially on my purpose and my growth areas. I then review any data that could inform the period I am reviewing (for example, my Safe Brave Space Tracker and/or previous reflection notes). Here's my simple framework:

DAILY REFLECTION (1 MINUTE)

- What was my personal safe brave action?
- How did it go? What worked well? What didn't?
- What's the most useful thing I learned today?
- What one thing will I do tomorrow to advance safe brave space?

WEEKLY REFLECTION (3–4 MINUTES)
- What progress did I make last week?
- What do I need to focus on in the coming week?
- Where are my key opportunities to advance SBS within me?

QUARTERLY REFLECTION (15–20 MINUTES)
- In the past three months, have I made the impact on myself, or in my relationships and in my world, to enable safe brave space?
- What are my key priorities for this coming quarter to enhance safe brave space?
- What do I need to do differently to achieve these priorities?
- Whom might I engage with to help me achieve my goals?

ANNUAL REFLECTION (1 HOUR)
- Once a year I take a deeper dive, reflecting on where I stand in regarding my life and the priorities that I have captured in my ME profile. From this reflection, I consider:
  o How have I strengthened my safe and brave muscles?
  o How has my growth helped enhance safe brave spaces around me?
  o Where do I want to be a year from now? What do I need to do or learn to get there?
  o What course corrections or changes do I need to implement this year to reach my goals?
  o What kind of support do I need from others, and where will I find it?

This Reflect, Recharge and Revise Framework is a powerful tool to hold ourselves accountable to our intentions and to create space to celebrate our traction along the way. With the insights from these reflection periods, we can update our ME profile and plan to meet the changes as we evolve our personal safe brave spaces.

Throughout this book I have stated that, as we begin the journey towards enabling safe brave spaces, we will see increased moments of joy, peace and freedom. Although I have defined what this means for me, it is also important to share the practical impact of investing the time and effort into "Starting within ME." The ROI of this work for me has been:

- Less time spent in spin, doubt and worry—studies show that 70 percent of our time is spent thinking about the past or the future, while the biggest impact we make is in the present.
- More opportunities aligned with my intentions—being more present and being clear of my commitments to cultivate and contribute has opened my eyes to see opportunities in front of me.
- Better sleep and more energy.
- Stronger confidence and commitment to Maximize Me.

Shifting how we more consistently Show Up requires us to establish good processes and test out new practices. The following questions will help you begin the journey and test out some tools and/or frameworks that resonate most in laying the foundations that will enhance your ability to Show Up more fully.

- What resonates most as "true" for you within this section? What most challenges and/or churns within you?
- Identify the area of Showing Up (Starting Strong; Stretching Often; Reflect, Recharge and Revise) that would be most valuable to advance.
- Select one exercise to try.
- Reflect on and capture any insights from this exercise.
- Update your Being ME profile and Safe Brave Plan with any insights.

Finalizing Your Being ME Profile and Safe Brave Plan

With the foundation of your Being ME Profile and Safe Brave Plan completed, the last step of this first stage of "Starting within ME" is to finalize the plan to advance both your safe and brave muscles. Leveraging the Being ME Profile and SBS Plan template found at www. safebravespaces.com—

1. Capture your SBS "current state" including where you are now, what has helped you get there, and what stands in the way of you becoming more safe and brave.
2. Review the insights from your Knowing, Growing, Letting Go and Showing Up work, and identify the single most important area of focus to release your personal contribution commitment and potential.
3. Identify two goals to strengthen your personal safe and brave space to enable the successful delivery of the priority area of focus identified in the previous point. Build a simple plan to attain your goals by answering the following questions:
   • What are my goals and why are they the most important?
   • What actions will I take to achieve them?
   • What does success look like?
   • Who can help me achieve it? (Hint … your inner circle/trusted community?)
4. Re-review the Showing Up section, especially the Reflect, Recharge and Revise discussion, and ensure you have a simple accountability plan to support your achievement.
5. Share all this with your inner circle and take the first step on your journey.

Getting real clarity around ME, including what you need to Let Go of and how you can best Show Up, is *so* important, as it provides the solid foundation and realization of the reality that it's not just about "me." Instead, safe brave spaces "accelerate between YOU and ME."

With a heightened state of being safe and brave within ourselves, we become more aware of external disruptions, most of which occur when we're with others. As almost everything happens "in-between," our enhanced personal safe and brave state equips us to help uncover and release this same state in others.

In the remainder of the book, we will explore ways to enhance safe brave spaces in both your one-on-one relationships (YOU & ME) and among your broader communities (WE). We will leverage the framework of Knowing, Growing, Letting Go, and Showing Up and provide practical insights and tools both to cultivate your relationships and enable the realization of your full potential through safe brave spaces.

4. Safe Brave Spaces Accelerates between YOU & ME

From an early age we realize that everything happens "in-between." The energy exchange that I spoke of earlier is most commonly found between two people, and this exchange can be both positive and negative. We see this truth both in science, most clearly through the study of magnetism, and personally in the multiple interactions we experience every day. The awareness uncovered within your ME Search, combined with the enhanced understanding of the power of pause and use of ELOPE, will better equip you as you explore and experience YOU & ME. An interesting awareness that I also discovered early on is that strengthening my "safe"—my awareness, confidence and trust in my truths and my gifts—and strengthening my "brave"—the courage to voice and contribute my truths and gifts—are both essential and yet have the possibility to increase disruption in my relationships. This disruption can be positive or negative. Increasing the likelihood of its being positive requires me to Know and Grow my understanding, trust and appreciation of others; to Let Go of the things that can impede those relationships; and to Show Up in various ways to enable safe brave spaces between myself and others.

To accomplish this, I needed to:

1. Strengthen my Ubuntu;
2. Understand the broader truth and story; and
3. Activate my inner child and awaken my warrior.

Strengthen My Ubuntu

Ubuntu is a South African term meaning someone who is "open and available to others, affirming of others, [and who] does not feel threatened that others are able and good." What Ubuntu underscores is "'the vital importance of mutual recognition and respect complemented by mutual care and sharing in the construction of human relations. Ubuntu is manifested in self-giving and readiness to cooperate and communicate with others." This term is at the core of enabling safe brave spaces within both my relationships and in the larger community.

A person who has a strong Ubuntu is someone who knows and lives a life based upon an abundance mindset as opposed to a scarcity mindset, and who commits to understanding and strengthening their emotional intelligence. A person with an abundance mindset believes that there is always more of everything in life, whether that's money, relationships, resources, opportunities, and so on. Alternatively, someone with a scarcity mentality lives in fear that they are going to lose their time or money. There is a big difference between the two mindsets. The path that your life takes depends, in part, on the mindset that you adopt. You can choose to view the world either way, but the two mindsets cannot coexist. The abundance mindset flows out of a deep inner sense of personal worth and security. It is a paradigm grounded in the belief that there is more than enough for everyone. Alternatively, a scarcity mindset is the belief that there will never be enough, resulting in feelings of fear, stress, and anxiety. In his book, *The Seven Habits of Highly Effective People*, Stephen Covey explains that when you live in a world of scarcity, you compete for available resources even when there is an abundance of them. A person who has a strong Ubuntu strives to live a life with an abundance mindset.

Enhanced emotional intelligence ("EI") is a second key attribute of a person with Ubuntu. I define emotional intelligence as a set of emotional and social skills that influence the way we perceive and express ourselves, develop and maintain social relationships, cope with challenges, and use emotional information in an effective and meaningful way. It is a key contributor to enabling safe brave spaces as people with higher EI form strong relationships and create powerful coping strategies. We can also measure emotional intelligence; doing so is less controversial than measuring IQs and unlike IQs, EI can be substantially strengthened and developed. There are several tools available that help individuals and teams understand and develop plans to enhance EI. The one I have found most valuable and provide for my clients is *EQi 2.0* from MHS. For more information on the tool, go to the SBS website.

The Broader Truth

The awareness of the importance of understanding others and being open to the broader truth is best captured in the famous proverb of the three vision-impaired friends describing their experience of an elephant. Each person is asked to describe the elephant. The first person, who is touching the trunk, describes the elephant as a large, thick snake. The second person, who is feeling the elephant's ear, describes it as a large fan. Finally, the third person, who is touching the elephant's sides, describes it as a wall. Each person's perception is accurate and provides an important view of the attributes of the elephant. As we learned in the exercises around biases, we too create a clear view of each situation we encounter and based on this view declare what is true for us. Just as with the three friends and the elephant, although our view may be true for us, there is a bigger, broader truth that we can only understand and experience when we are open to the truths of others.

Being open to the broader truth is easier said than done, especially when we feel that our core values or purpose are being infringed upon. I am certain we have all experienced the visceral reaction when confronting an equally powerful position and passion expressed by another person. For me it is almost as if I have been transported into a *Star Wars* movie and I am experiencing the power of the Force. Depending on who it is and how much that other viewpoint aligns to my own values and purpose, that force is either Darth Vader or Luke Skywalker. In either case, we need to heed Yoda's wise counsel to Luke to "use the Force," or what we have been describing throughout this book as the power to pause, ELOPE and SAIL towards your own deeper wisdom and the wisdom of others.

Activating My Inner Child and Awakening My Warrior

The last component is the process I call "activating my inner child and awakening my warrior." I recently found a book that my mother had given my siblings and me for Christmas when we were all in our early thirties. The book is a collection of pictures from when we were born until our mid-twenties. It was such a lovely gift, one which automatically evoked splendid memories of—and emotions around—past events and experiences. One of the biggest insights that struck me as I looked at the pictures was the sense of wonder and curiosity in my face as a child. Particularly in the early years up until age four or five, there seemed to be a peaceful, transparent, loving energy that shone from the page. It led me to think we are born innocent, with this beautiful gift of wonder and openness. Depending on our childhood situation, this lasts for at least a few years. I recognize that I am truly blessed to have had my parents, who even during some challenging times held the space open for me to experience this wonder. It strikes me now that they exhibited an authentic example of enabling safe space. As I reflected on these pictures, in particular one of me at age four, I realized that this wonder and openness was still in me and that I could rediscover and reactivate my inner child. This is a process that started with one simple step. With my phone, I took a picture of the original photo and placed a copy in three strategic locations: on the edge of my computer monitor, in the front of my journal (with my ME Profile), and on my computer so it would show up occasionally as my screen saver. On the top of each photo are the words "Activate my inner child." Earlier, I shared the importance of starting strong to help us show up. It has shocked me how seeing my four-year-old self and choosing to activate his perspective has enhanced my ability to be more safe and to create a safer space for others.

The notion of awakening my warrior also evolved from those pictures. Besides the sense of wonder and openness, in the eyes of my young self there seemed to be a glimmer or spark indicating that I was ready and willing to jump into anything. Although I believe that desire has always been in me, I recognize now that my instincts for optimism, community and peacemaking had become overemphasized to the point where my "brave" was much more underdeveloped than my "safe." This isn't necessarily bad as it is a key gift that I bring; however, it isn't all that I am, and awakening the warrior within would further enhance my potential and my ability to support others in finding their safe brave space.

It was at this point that I discovered the second picture that I posted alongside my childhood photo. This came about through spending time with my daughter Danica.

Earlier in my career I travelled a lot, which unfortunately resulted in me not being as present as I might have been with my kids early in their lives. I always made it a priority to spend time with family when I was home, but I recognize now that often my spouse and kids got the short end of the stick when it came to my time. During their teens and twenties, I made a conscious effort to spend more quality time with both my son and daughter, and it was during one of those times that I discovered a fictional person who helped awaken my inner warrior. Her name is Xena. I suspect that isn't the first name that you thought I would pick, but Danica helped me see that Xena was in fact the perfect person to stir and solidify what a warrior looked like for me. At her foundation, Xena emulates strength, vulnerability and community. These qualities are not only aligned with my values and purpose but also are key to accelerating safe brave spaces between YOU & ME.

Accelerating safe brave spaces between YOU & ME occurs when I enhance my one-on-one relationships. I found that the phases we worked through in our personal re-discovery were equally effective in this stage of the journey. Knowing and Growing allow us to enrich safe muscles and spaces between us, laying the foundation to enable us to be brave individually and in relationships. Letting Go and Showing Up equip us to release the brave between us and further advance the safe. This momentum deepens our individual wisdom and advances our collective potential.

Knowing, within the context of YOU & ME, begins with our belief in the power of synergy and is revealed through a desire to understand, value and trust in the opportunity to learn from others' unique perspectives and contributions.

Pulling It All Together:
Creating Your YOU & ME Profile and SBS Plan

As with the ME stage, as you complete the Knowing phase of understanding YOU & ME, you may find it helpful to create a simple summary for easy reference of what you have discovered about each other and how together you are committed to enabling safe brave spaces within your relationship. This double-sided, one-sheet document is similar to the "Being ME" Profile and SBS Plan, and can become a valuable tool that you can tweak as your relationship grows. You can find the YOU & ME Profile template at www.safebravespaces.com.

knowing

Knowing YOU & ME

Earlier in the book, when I introduced the pathway to ELOPE, I noted that in the final stage—*Engage*—we become more deeply connected not only to our inner selves but to those around us. Knowing between YOU & ME is about seeing those connections and uncovering unique perspectives and contributions in them. The simplest way that I have found to summarize that process is to *Care, Share and Declare.*

Caring is the springboard to accelerating safe brave spaces between YOU & ME. The good news is that, if you have already chosen to ELOPE, you are entering the connection with a mindset of love, gratitude and openness. This, combined with a strengthening Ubuntu, a curiosity about the broader truth and partnering with your inner child and warrior, will create the needed safe space to explore each other. This is most important and impactful the more diverse the participants' experiences.

The second component, *Sharing*, will require each of you to tap into both your safe and brave muscles. It involves stating your intentions for the dialogue and your mutual commitment to understanding each other's values, gifts, passions, purpose and perspectives. Beginning by sharing your intentions is critical because there can be a sizeable gap between intention and impact. Some of the biggest misses in my life have resulted from my failure to share my intentions, not being clear about them, or not taking the time to understand the intentions of others.

I have come to realize that people can't read my mind; that's why it is so important to be clear about my intentions, especially at the beginning of a new relationship. Once you have aligned on intention and commitment, you can then begin the discovery process. If this is a new relationship some or all of the following questions can help kick-start the dialogue:

1. What is most important to you and why (passions, priorities)?
2. What are the values and supporting behaviours present in your strongest partnerships/relationships?
3. What unique gifts, experiences, skills and attributes have you and/or others recognized as your strengths that could maximize the success of our relationship?
4. What differing gifts, experience, skills and attributes do you most need to leverage from others?

If either of you have previously completed more detailed ME work, I would encourage you to bring those insights to the dialogue. Often, I have started the discussion by sharing my ME profile and my Safe Brave Plan as they provide a useful framework and enable openness through vulnerability.

The third component, *Declaring*, is about providing each other greater clarity around how you work and uncovering some important "need-to-know" facts that will facilitate healthy dialogue. Some of the biggest hindrances in relationships stem from lack of understanding of how the other person works. Tools such as Kolbe, the enneagram, EQi.2.0 and DISC provide some insights and language that can support this part of the dialogue. If possible, invest in a mutually agreed upon tool, as this allows for common language and shared understandings. I have discovered the importance of this point both professionally and personally. My wife Josette is someone who is very organized and planful person. She is a realist who appreciates receiving information ahead of time to enable reflective analysis to support decision-making. I am someone who is very fluid, less structured, and who can quickly pull what I believe are the critical data points to move forward. As well, I am an optimist who appreciates the use of "executive summaries" and creative brainstorming to support decision-making. Lack of understanding of how we both work can quickly lead to conflict and a drop in the levels of both safe and brave. Clarity and honouring each other's "how," especially the ways in which we are different, is a beautiful thing and from a personal perspective has resulted in thirty-three years of mostly heavenly bliss. Within a work context, lack of clarity and appreciation of how others work is the single most impactful hindrance to improving relationships.

Accelerating safe brave spaces between YOU & ME can be overwhelming as we have so many relationships and connections in our lives. The following questions will help you reflect on where to begin and to test out some tools and/or frameworks for advancing safe brave spaces within one-to-one relationships.

- What resonates most as "true" for you within this section? What most challenges and/or churns within you?
- Identify one person with whom you would like to accelerate safe brave spaces.

- Capture who they are, why they are important to you and what a "best friend" would look like.
- Select one exercise to share with them and experiment
- Reflect on and capture any insights you are learning from this exercise.

Growing YOU & ME

A commitment to knowing each other is an important first step and the springboard to advance trust, a critical ingredient in realizing our collective potential. In this stage, Growing is about investing in, accepting, **growing** loving, valuing and expanding this understanding of YOU & ME. It is about establishing a plan to apply the new insights that we have discovered about each other and cultivating a healthier and more impactful relationship. To recap what I discussed earlier in the book, everything is energy, and humans are the greatest source of energy. When energy collides there is disruption, sometimes positive and sometimes negative. Key to a Growing plan is to build attributes and frameworks to predict and manage those disruptions and channel the energy into productive pathways. The good news is that many of the ideas, tools and frameworks that we applied within the ME chapters will also support YOU & ME. To better understand what we need, it is first important to understand what we are growing: *trust*.

Although there are many formulas for trust, the one I like the best is from a book called *The Trusted Advisor* by David H. Maister, Charles H. Green and Robert M. Galford. It is simple to understand and easy to apply. Their "Trust Equation" is:

Trust = Credibility + Reliability + Intimacy/ Self Orientation

In their book the authors suggest that there are four primary components of trustworthiness having to do with words, actions, emotions and motives. To grow trust between each other, you need to be advancing all four dimensions.

Credibility is the aspect of trust that is most commonly achieved and is both about content expertise and "presence." You must not only be credible, but the other person must *see* that you are credible. I believe that credibility is earned over time and is grounded in accuracy, confidence in knowledge, and honesty.

The second component, *reliability*, is rooted in your being dependable and trusted to behave in consistent ways. Perception of your level of reliability is strongly affected, if not determined, by the number of times someone interacts with you. Reliability in a rational sense is the repeated correlation of promises and actions, and from an emotional perspective is the repeated experience of expectations fulfilled.

Intimacy is described as one of the most effective and common sources of differentiation in levels of trustworthiness. It is also the area where we most commonly fail in trust building. People trust those with whom they will talk about any situation, including difficult topics. Intimacy within the context of this trust equation is about emotion, not physical connectivity, and requires heightened emotional intelligence. Relationships strong in this component enjoy greater levels of safe and brave spaces.

The last component, *self-orientation*, is about the balance between YOU & ME and, like intimacy, is a key differentiator in trustworthiness. Individuals with a strong sense of self combined with a propensity towards other-centredness embody a level of self-orientation that increases trust. A healthy plan to grow YOU & ME will include commitments and actions that increase credibility, reliability and intimacy, all of which help to balance self-orientation. Two of the best ways to accomplish this are to identify and address the things that might get in the way of the relationship, and to cultivate things that can increase trust.

If intimacy and self-orientation are the biggest differentiators in building trust, our opportunity is to discover practices and tools to help strengthen these qualities within our relationships. If intimacy is strengthened by enhancing emotional connection, vulnerability and transparency, these become key ingredients in building safe brave spaces. With the foundation of the "knowing" work now laid, we can share and explore the things that get in our way. As we discovered in the ME work, the things that often impede YOU & ME bubble up out of our individual fears, biases and privilege. When we connect with others, matters can sometimes get complicated as a result of the diversity of our experiences, something which is at the core of fears and biases. During this stage, increased levels of safe and brave provide a pathway to share some of these more difficult insights. Declaring your known biases and blind spots is a critical step to enable growth between YOU & ME. Within the ME chapter we outlined several ways to uncover your fears, biases, privileges and blind spots. Vulnerability is key in enabling you to declare what you discovered within yourself, how you are responding to your insights, and enrolling the other person in helping you shift. This step requires each person to be even more brave. Prior to this discussion, it is important for each person to have done some work in identifying those things that may get in the way. Tools such as the enneagram, when completed by each person, provide shared language to deepen awareness and understanding of each other including important areas such as fears, triggers and pathways to growth. Ideally, working through the ME exercise as a baseline will provide helpful foundational insights for this dialogue. That being said, the following questions, even without the pre-work, are useful thought-starters to help each of you identify the things that might hinder safe brave spaces between you and create common commitments to support their growth. I recommend first completing them individually and then sharing your insights with one another.

1. When reflecting upon my relationship with others:
    a. The blind spots that sometimes get me in trouble are…
    b. The strengths that I can sometimes overuse are…
    c. The knowledge gaps that I know exist in me are…
    d. The fears and unconscious biases that sometimes hinder my ability to more fully show up are…
2. The three development areas that I am working on to strengthen my relationships with others are…
3. The way you can support me in our relationship is…

The second differentiator, self-orientation, is about finding that balance in YOU & ME. It is about creating a space for the emergence of both the safe and the brave for one another. It requires each person to hold an abundance mindset and to commit to strengthening two key attributes: curiosity and courage. Curiosity is defined as a desire to know, an inquisitive interest in other's concerns. Stephen Covey suggests that it requires us to "seek first to understand prior to being understood." This can be challenging, in particular when what the other person is saying clashes with our core beliefs or values. Building curiosity is the key to move beyond "my truth" to see "the broader truth" and to help enable safe spaces. Courage is defined as the mental or moral strength to venture, persevere, and withstand danger, fear, or difficulty. For us to more fully show up and contribute to any relationship, we have to trust our instincts and speak our truths. Doing so requires us to tap into our inner warrior and release our brave.

Developing and maintaining trust is difficult when you experience the energy surges that naturally occur when two varying perspectives collide. Even with some splendid work within the Knowing phase, I guarantee you that disruptions, both positive and negative, will still occur. The last component of Growing is noticing those disruptions, and as in our individual work, finding ways to better channel the energy towards something more positive and effective.

Understanding the Energy of YOU & ME

Earlier I introduced the Energy Exploration Exercise (EEE). This simple journaling exercise is a great tool to track the energy flow between two people. As with any good journaling process, it provides a platform for dialogue to understand and enhance how you work together. Simply track the energy spikes when you meet and capture the answers to the following questions.

1. When we connect, what are the energy surges that we sense and where do they show up?
2. What are the feelings that each of us experience when they happen (i.e., excitement, anger, annoyance, joy)?

3. What does it make each of us want to do? (How do I want to respond?)
4. What can we learn from this and what might we change or shift in future connections?

Reviewing your journal after a couple of weeks will help you identify some actions and triggers that result in energy surges between you. Recognizing and exploring the themes and patterns will help you better to predict and prevent potential negative disruptions. The insights and ideas combined with those uncovered through both the knowing and growing phase will strengthen your understanding and appreciation of each other, which will enhance your collective safe brave space. I have also found that, as your relationship strengthens, you will be more comfortable sharing when the energy boost is occurring during your conversations. A simple approach that I have found helpful to do this is to simply declare:

•   That "something is bubbling up for you" or "I am experiencing one of those energy surges";
•   That "something about our discussion is making me feel ——, which is resulting in me..."
•   "Are you sensing anything? Can we explore this further?"

By taking the time to notice these situations and explore the impact, you will have greater success at Letting Go.

Growing safe brave spaces between YOU & ME begins through the enhancement of mutual trust. The following questions will help you collectively reflect on where you are and test out some tools and/or frameworks to advance this important foundation of relationships.

- What resonates most as "true" for you within this section? What most challenges and/or churns within you?
- With either the person you have been working with or someone else with whom you have begun deepening safe brave spaces,
  - o Select one exercise within this section to deepen your relationship and collective SBS; and
  - o Reflect on and capture any insights you are learning.

● **letting go**

Letting Go of What Hinders YOU & ME

When we make a commitment to knowing and growing together, we strengthen our collective trust and appreciation of each other. Stephen Covey describes this process as building up deposits in your trust bank. This accumulation of trust is important, especially when we experience negative disruptors within our relationships. Some of these disruptors result from external forces unrelated to our relationship or situation, but that makes them no less impactful. Often, they are created by ME, most often unintentionally, and yet can quickly send a dialogue or relationship into a spin. Even after developing a better understanding of others and committing to entering each interaction with the intention of maximizing positive energy, love and potential, I have found myself bewildered by how my responses can set a relationship back. I have discovered over and over that intention and impact are two very different things. Often I have entered a conversation with the best of intentions only to leave with significant injury to both myself and others. Even entering and declaring good intentions does not guarantee that I won't stumble, especially when experiencing different truths and with external pressures surging. In these moments, I recognize the need to cultivate the ability to Let Go.

Triggers to Truths

As suggested earlier, in a world of "in-between" we are bound to experience energy disruptions when we run into others with both similar and different experiences, beliefs, truths, and filters. These disruptions can be positive or negative, for us personally and for others. The key is knowing what, when and how to Let Go.

For me, it begins by recognizing my triggers—the early warning signs of disruption. Triggers show up in different ways for different people. Thinkers hear them in their heads, feelers connect to their hearts and doers feel them first in their bodies. We all access our whole selves both to take note of triggers and manage our energy bursts, including the most undeveloped and important fourth component, the "gut" (aka our inner wisdom). As I've shared many times before, I am definitely a "thinker" who tends to get lost in my head. Leveraging my meditation practices and the Energy Exploration Exercise, I am becoming more successful in creating that pause required to more effectively and compassionately respond to the energy disruptions. The physical triggers that I experience because of these surges—the tingly or flushed skin, tense muscles, and rubbing of hands—are the same whether the work at hand involves just ME or YOU & ME. But the stories and critics that emerge in these situations are sometimes different. When disruption occurs in my relationships, in addition to the "me-critic" the "you-critics" also arrive. These critics come equipped with envy, judgement, pride, stubbornness, and impatience. They believe they are protecting me but in fact impede my one-on-one relationships. They are driven primarily by my privilege, my biases and my fears. Key for me is finding avenues to both remind myself of the existence of these culprits and find pathways to move beyond them.

This begins with sensing the energy surges between me and the other person, something I do by leveraging my learning from my meditation and breathing exercises. Taking three deep breaths or sometimes writing the word "breathe" in my journal is enough to create a pause. In that moment of pause, I have learned to access the ELOPE pathway to get me to a place where I can see what is true in the moment and silence the you-critics. I begin by recognizing:

- E > The **energy** shift, and naming what I am feeling in the moment. Normally, it includes anger, annoyance, judgement or envy towards the other person or what they have said. Verbalizing the positive or negative emotions helps deepen the pause and reminds me to shift to Love.
- L > When I choose to experience the situation through the eyes of **Love,** gratitude, mercy, empathy and compassion, I accept and acknowledge the potential of a hidden "gift" in either the situation or in the person whom I am interacting with . Studies have proven that our human instincts are built to react, and these reactions inform us. When I proactively look for and am grateful for the person, the situation and/or the conversation, I open myself to what is happening in the moment.
- O > Through the eyes of Love I enable **Openness,** widening my curiosity and wonder. Thus I am more likely to investigate both my reaction and the potential gift or learning being provided. With this broadening view I am also able to acknowledge my wider experience with this individual.
- P > In this state of Openness, I can be more **Present** to what is true and untrue in this moment. With a clearer head I can tap into that deeper wisdom and see my desires, feelings, memories and experiences, enhancing my discernment and decision-making.
- E > When I am more Present, I can more fully **Engage** and connect. With a clearer, deeper view and heightened discernment, I see alternative channels for the energy. This helps me see more productive ways to respond to a situation.

When I arrive at the second **E,** Engage, I am better able to tap into my deeper wisdom and more open to connect to the other person's perspective. It also allows me to more easily activate my inner child and awaken my inner warrior, two key resources to manage the critics, Let Go of untruths, and widen my view to encompass broader truths. Through this process the composition of my energy shifts from negative to positive, the accompanying emotions from anger, annoyance, judgement or envy towards gratefulness, curiosity, openness. These shifts re-establish the foundations to re-enable safe brave spaces.

Holding openness is one of the most difficult things for me to do, especially when a core truth or belief is being challenged. My learned behaviour is to defend my truth and the most powerful weapon on my belt is judgment. Even when I leverage ELOPE, there have still been times when I find I quickly shift back to a locked-in position that starts to re-energize the spin cycle. Byron Katie provides a list of some simple questions in her book *Loving What Is* that have always been helpful for me as I probe my heart in these situations. She suggests when we find ourselves in this spin cycle—whether the target is ourselves or others—that we first write down our stressful thoughts, and then ask ourselves the following four questions about the statements we have written down.

- **Question 1:** Is it true? > This question can change your life. Be still and ask yourself if the thought you wrote down really is true.
- **Question 2:** Can you absolutely know it's true? > This is another opportunity to open your mind and to go deeper into the unknown, to find the answers that live beneath what we think we know.
- **Question 3:** How do you react—what happens—when you believe that thought is true? > With this question, you begin to notice internal cause and effect. You can see that when you believe the statement, there is a disturbance that can range from mild discomfort to fear or panic. What do you feel? How do you treat the person (or the situation) you've written about when you believe that thought? How do you treat yourself? Make a list and be specific.
- **Question 4:** Who would you be without the thought? > Imagine yourself in the presence of that person (or in that situation), without believing the thought you've written down. How would your life be different if you did not even *think* the stressful thought? How would you feel? Which do you prefer—life with or without the thought? Which feels kinder, more peaceful?

She then suggests that we **turn the thought around.** This "turn-around" gives you an opportunity to broaden your perspective by re-writing your original statements and simply replacing the "he/she/they" with "I." In other words, make the statement about you, not the other person. Once you have found one or more turnarounds to your original statement, you are invited to find at least three specific, genuine examples of how each turnaround is true in your life.

The majority of the time when I walk through these questions, I discover that either my thought is not true or that the thought is impacting me and limiting both my potential and the collective potential more than it is helping. This realization helps to maintain and often expand my openness to the situation and supports my inner explorer. In this mindset I can more easily springboard off her last question to investigate the broader truth, the gift in the moment. Letting go of the tight grip on my truth allows me to become more curious and interested in the insights and perspectives of others. It returns me to a place of engagement and connection with the other person. Connection is about finding common bridges between us and enhancing our desire to understand the other person's experience, which has helped form their perspective. It is amazing how, entering a conversation with a greater sense of openness, we so often find areas of agreement and shared experience that we previously hadn't discovered. It's much like the frantic experience of trying to find a lost set of keys. When I can calm down and Let Go, I often discover that the keys are right in front of me. The same is true in working with others. I am convinced that all of us have something in common and that only through openness and a curious spirit can we find bridges between us.

By now you will notice that I am a big proponent of the power of questions to deepen understanding as they can strengthen the connectivity which helps accelerate safe brave spaces. Within these spaces we open up and gain access to that reservoir of internal wisdom and a desire to seek the wisdom of others. When we collectively tap into this space, our individual and collective potential expands. When I find myself in this heightened state of connection the following questions have been helpful in exploring that wider truth and wisdom.

- Tell me about the experiences that helped form your thinking.
- Within those experiences, what were your biggest insights and why?
- What else might help me more deeply understand your perspective?

This past August I had the opportunity to apply these two approaches in a work context. I experienced one of these energy surges after sending a blog entry in for peer review by my partners. One partner sent a short note back suggesting that we should post it and that they expected some people wouldn't like it. Besides the fact I perceived the reply as a negative comment, to add to the churn I received the response after completing nine holes of golf with my son Jenssen (the first time I had seen him in person for a long time because of Covid-19 restrictions) in 35-degree-Celsius heat. In the moment I could feel the you-critics gathering and the negative energy swirling at an increased speed, immediately beginning to disrupt this awesome moment of reconnection with my son. Fortunately, my insightful son asked a simple question: "Hey, Dad, is everything okay?" This created a chance for me to pause. An expression of love, through a caring question, has amazing power. In that moment, I took three deep breaths and walked through the model. I chose to ELOPE:

- E > Recognize and name the **Energy** shift. In this case, with regard to the partner's feedback, it was annoyance and anger. Recognizing this internal negative churn reminded me to re-examine this situation through the lens of Love.
- L > Experience it through the eyes of **Love,** gratitude, mercy, empathy and compassion. I reminded myself that my business partner has always been supportive, I valued their experience, they had often respectfully challenged me to enhance my thinking, and I have learned much from their past advice.
- O > This re-examination through a lens of love enabled more **Openness,** curiosity and wonder. The love and gratitude caused me to widen my view and become curious about what they may have been trying to say.

- P > In this state of Openness, I become more **Present**, choosing to let go of the you-critics and better able to tap into my deeper wisdom and access my partner's insights. This choice calmed my mind storm, got me further excited about understanding their insights, and helped me return to the positive moment with my son.
- E > When I become more Present, I became more fully **Engaged** and connected, helping me see a clear pathway forward, including setting up a call to seek first to understand.

In that call, which occurred later that afternoon and which I entered into with a spirit of curiosity, I leveraged the three questions above and discovered that the partner's primary concern was that I hadn't connected the blog post with an obvious example to help others apply the model. It was an amazing insight that strengthened the blog considerably. This insight would had been lost had I not found a different pathway to see the broader truth. An additional benefit was the shift that occurred in the connection with my son for the final nine holes of the golf game. His expression of care through his question combined with my choosing to Let Go of the negative disruption somehow deepened our connection at the moment. Our conversation shifted from general topics to deeper things we were each experiencing in the quarantine. There was an immediate acceleration of the safe and brave space between us, which resulted in one of the best dialogues we have had in a considerable time.

Leveraging these approaches can also be equally effective in our personal lives. A case where I experienced the power of choosing to ELOPE in my personal relationships came during a recent trip to South Africa.

In the fall of 2019, I had the wonderful opportunity to attend an enneagram conference in Cape Town and planned a three-day stay at an animal reserve in the country's north along the border of Botswana. My wife, who could not attend the conference, had entrusted my safety to my sister and my brother-in-law. To provide some context, I do have a history of naivety when exploring areas that may not be the safest, something which has left me on more than one occasion close to death. All was going smoothly until the second day of our stay at the animal reserve when a storm arose while we were out with the trackers late in the afternoon. We had heard a white rhino and some cheetahs were close by and were heading to their last reported location. I was in my glory, amazed by the beauty around me and grateful for this opportunity to experience the splendid work that this organization was doing for the preservation of these magnificent animals. In the midst of the drive, the winds picked up and heavy storm clouds began gathering to the east. This was an amazing sight, and the promise of rain was very exciting for a community that had had no precipitation for over a year. Within thirty minutes it started to rain. Fortunately, we were equipped with ponchos and continued our exploration through the reserve. As the rain intensified and the lightning (which was spectacular) began, our driver stopped the vehicle and asked whether we wanted to continue. My first reaction—"We are in a vehicle with rubber tires and I am certain that we are safe, or they wouldn't have given us the option"—was seconded by the other family in our vehicle. The adventure would continue, and my energy soared until my sister, who is as adventurous or more than me, stated, "I think we should return to the lodge."

This is the point where I should have been grateful to my loving sister—who was fulfilling my wife's request—graciously acknowledged her concerns and agreed to return to the lodge. Unfortunately, my negative triggers kicked in. I took the opposite pathway, toward annoyance and defensiveness. I dug into my position and reiterated that we should continue and "monitor things." My sister agreed, and we continued for another ten minutes during which the lightning and rain intensified, finally leaving me no choice but to agree to return to the lodge. I knew my sister's intentions and should have been grateful, but after we had been dropped off and the driver headed back out to the reserve with the other family, my internal energy and emotions churned and brewed like a volcano about the erupt. This would have been a beautiful opportunity to pause and be grateful for my caring sister. I chose door number two, shoved my feelings down and pretended that all was well.

Act two of this personal learning experience occurred as we sat on the lodge's porch, having a glass of wine, watching the beautiful lightning strikes across the plain, and listening to the sounds of nature. My sister opened her computer, read articles out loud and got distracted with what I considered "busyness." This action, not unusual for my sister who is a trailblazer, highly curious and whom I admire greatly, normally draws me in and gets me equally excited. In my current state, it irritated me and stirred the molten frustration that was building within. The truth that echoed in my head was "How can she be wasting time on a computer when we are surrounded by such beauty?" Fortunately, the work I had been doing around knowing and growing YOU & ME helped remind me that this was an opportunity to ELOPE.

- E—As I sat on the chair I acknowledged that I was frustrated, angry at being limited, envious of those still on safari and judgmental of what I perceived as my sister and brother-in-law being overly fearful. Forcing myself to name my feelings enabled me to pause. In that moment, coincidentally, there was a nearby lightning strike, which created a shift to re-examine through Love.
- L—As I turned towards the lightning, I saw my sister and brother-in-law sitting next to me. In that moment, I saw the excitement on their faces and recognized that my sister loved me and she was simply fulfilling a commitment to my wife. This led to a deeper sense of gratefulness for family and a recognition that they were always there for me. This shift allowed me to be more open to the situation.
- O—In a more Open state, I could see what was true and what was untrue. They weren't limiting me; they were trying to protect me, and they cared deeply for me and I for them.
- P—The openness allowed me to become more Present in the truth of this moment and tap into my deeper awareness within myself, and the experiences that the three of us had shared over the past thirty-five years. This further deepened gratitude and allowed my head to clear and become more engaged with alternative pathways.

- E—In that moment I wasn't perfectly settled; however, I was more mindful of my choices. Tapping into my deeper instincts, I experience a deep sense of peace and I quietly excused myself, moving to the second floor of the lodge for some quiet meditation.

Sitting in a chair on the deck, I focused on slowing my breath, took in the amazing view and began reflecting on the gift of this trip, my family and the world around me. Instantly the final bits of my frustrations slipped away, and a sense of peace overwhelmed me. Curiously enough, as soon as I settled into this state, I heard my sister call my name inquiring where I was and within five minutes the three of us were gathered together, arms locked on a couch, silently enveloped in the moment's beauty. Finding a better way to leverage my energy and to channel it towards something good had transformed what could have been a time of sped-up negative emotion, anger and regret to one of shared joy and peace. As I sat in my room later that evening I reflected on the situation's wasted energy, missed opportunities and hindered potential that had been mitigated through the application of a couple of simple tools to learn to more quickly Let Go.

We have talked about the impact and ways to let go of the "you-critics" that hinder relationships. Before turning to Showing Up, it is also important to restate that self-critics can be equally harmful to YOU & ME as they hinder my brave. To be fully present in my relationship and support the potential of others, it is important for me to share my truths, especially when I sense my perspective could help the other person see a broader truth. The need to be brave in these kinds of situations has been heightened recently as we have witnessed demonstrations against systemic racism around the world. I have been doing a lot of listening to friends within the BIPOC community and reflecting about where my silence in conversation, driven by fear, has exacerbated the situation within my circle of influence. I recognize that, as an ally, I need to enhance my brave and more courageously support the required shift beginning with each conversation. One first step I am taking comes from a wonderful book called *So You Want to Talk About Race* by Ijeomo Oluo. When

I find myself in conversations where someone shares misinformation and/or concerning statements, I am no longer silent and more consistently state "that is not my experience" followed by factual information that I have discovered through listening and research. As we enhance safe brave spaces between YOU & ME, we build trust, which helps us recognize and Let Go of the things that impede fully releasing our individual and collective courage to kindly and directly help each other shift to the broader truth and more consistently Show Up.

Letting Go of behaviours that hinder our relationships is both a difficult and highly rewarding step in the journey. The following questions will help you collectively identify potential barriers and test out some tools and/or frameworks to help you release the things that are hindering your relationships in this moment.

- What resonates most as "true" for you within this section? What most challenges and/or churns within you?
- Review any previous work around fears, biases or privilege.
- Reflect on this work: what surprised you, what "you-critics" have you discovered, and what most hinders you from enabling safe brave spaces in your one-to-one relationships?
- Select one exercise or tool to begin Letting Go of that hindrance. Share your intention with the person with whom you are in relationship.
- Reflect on and capture any insights you are learning from this exercise.

Showing Up Fully between YOU & ME

Showing Up is about preparing for and leveraging the learnings and awareness to enable
safe brave spaces in every moment. As with
the first three components, I have discovered
some additional insights that help me do this
more consistently.

 showing up

Most of the interactions and energy disruptions that occur during
the day are unplanned. Time is almost always at a premium—except,
perhaps, during such unusual situations as the Covid-19 lockdowns,
and even then many people, and especially those in front-line positions, have been busier than ever—and we pack our days full, which
leaves us little time to find space to think about, much less prepare
for, Showing Up. Unfortunately, all our well-planned intentions can
falter if we don't reflect on and implement ways of enhancing how we
Show Up. Throughout my life there have been many occasions when
I have entered a meeting or conversation with the best of intentions
and even left feeling that I had really "nailed it" only to discover later
that the actual impact was far removed from my intention. As Robin
Hood pointed out, "If you don't take the time to aim your shot, missing by an inch at release can mean a miss by a yard at the ultimate
target." If you don't take the time to reflect upfront, you will miss the
target.

Showing Up requires me to pause and to access my energy and
intentions before entering a conversation. I have found that I increase
the likelihood of Showing Up and have healthier dialogues with others when I proactively focus on the same three steps employed in the
ME exercises we discussed earlier: Start Strong, Stretching Often, and
Reflect, Recharge, Revise.

Starting Strong

Starting Strong for me is more than having the factual knowledge required to be a full participant in my relationships and in each interaction. Within the context of Showing Up, Starting Strong embod-
ies preparedness, especially of my mindset and awareness. It is about

reflecting upon what we need to consider and how we want to enter each situation where we connect with others. An excellent illustration of this insight is found in a well-known story of a gorilla researcher who for weeks had made many failed attempts to enter a gorilla settlement. Each time she approached the gorillas she was met with opposition and prevented from getting close. After multiple attempts using various proven methods, she went to sleep exhausted and dejected. Early the next morning she woke from a fitful night with an insight that gave her immediate clarity around the situation. In each prior attempt, armed guides that had been provided for her protection had accompanied her. She realized that by taking this approach, her mindset while entering the camp was one of fear and caution. The gorillas, sensing this energy, responded in a protective and defensive fashion. In that moment, prior to the rest of the camp waking, she left on her own, unarmed, towards the gorilla settlement. As she approached the gorillas with a mindset of openness and curiosity they immediately welcomed her into the community without opposition.

Like the researcher, I know that I often enter an interaction with a mindset that is not open to listening and connecting. A poor start to my day, the nature of the meeting I just left, or possibly a previous conversation with the person I'm to meet with—all these things may get in the way. As a result, I have found blocking off five to ten minutes prior to the meeting to pause and proactively think about where I am and how I want to show up is extremely valuable. To help me more consistently do this, I have created what I call my ME & YOU "pre-checks."

In those cases where an interaction is not pre-planned and comes as a surprise, it's important to remember that we always have the choice of how we respond. Respectfully saying "Can you just give me ten minutes to finish something off and I'll give you my full attention" will allow you to quickly walk through the pre-check and set you and the other person up for a greater likelihood of success.

Pre-check #1: The "MEcheck"

Earlier, I spoke about the importance of our mindsets in the success of any interaction. We define mindset as mental attitude or inclination, a fixed state of mind. Mindset is something that is fully within our control and can be activated and managed using pause leveraging tools such as SAIL. Establishing a habit of leveraging the MEcheck forces us to acknowledge and reconnect to the reality of our own truths and untruths and role within the "in-between." These three quick questions help ground me in a more proactive mindset prior to a meeting:

1. What do I think, feel and sense about this situation or person?
2. What do I need to Let Go of that could inhibit a successful outcome?
3. What is the one thing I need to do to help enable a successful outcome?

Once I have completed the MEcheck I shift to the second pre-check—the "YOUcheck."

Pre-check #2: The "YOUcheck"

This second check allows you to access all the work that you have completed in Knowing, Growing and Letting Go. It is based on a model called CPR. I love the fact the model is called CPR as that is more commonly known as a technique to restart the heart, which curiously enough is exactly what this pre-check is metaphorically intended to do. Personally, I recognize when I am busy and under stress that I lose my sense of community and return to the mind storms. The YOUcheck is all about shifting from my perspective to understanding the perspective of the other person. The three components of CPR are Context, Purpose, and Results.

Context is about putting yourself in the other person's shoes to gain perspective before heading into a dialogue. During your pre-check time, think about the environment and context that the other person is coming from. Ask yourself:

•   What is going on—what other things are happening that might impact your conversation—and how ready are they to hear it?
•   Who will be there and what do they expect?
•   What has previously been shared on this topic?

Clarity around the **purpose** of your meeting needs to be established and articulated prior to starting the meeting. Be clear on what you want to communicate, how you want to communicate, and what is your desired impact. It is equally important to consider what you think they expect to hear and want to hear.

The last component, **results**, is self-explanatory and unveiled by answering the following questions:

- What does success look like?
- What do I/they need to walk away with?
- How do you want people to feel?

I cannot emphasize enough the importance and impact of taking ten minutes prior to any interaction to conduct a MEcheck and YOUcheck. I guarantee that besides preparing your heart and mind, opening up a positive learning environment will enhance both your conversations and the potential of each "in-between" interaction.

Stretching Often

The second step in enabling more consistent ways of Showing Up between YOU & ME is to stretch often. Your pre-check work will be an enormous boost in helping ensure that you remain flexible and focused; however, there is still the risk of becoming distracted and disrupted within your connection. Personally, along with my innate capacities of creativity, positivity and optimism comes what some call a "monkey mind." This is the other side of the coin that can impede me fully Showing Up with others. Sometimes I am distracted by other things on my mind; sometimes the cause is my desire to bring my wisdom and experience to bear on the person with whom I am meeting. Either way, it distracts me from being fully present and maximizing the meeting's potential.

Being present begins with eliminating as many distractions as possible. This includes the environment that you establish for the connection and the behaviours you exhibit within the dialogue. Simple things involving the environment include finding a private place where you can be focused and won't be interrupted. Turning our phones on silent mode and/or putting them away sends a very visual message that this conversation is important, and that you are prioritizing the time together. Ensuring the do-not-disturb sign is on the door and booking sufficient time for the dialogue are also important components of enabling your ability to be present. One of my favourite ways to help enable presence was originally shared with me by one of my friends. He begins each of his interactions with a minute of silence. He explains to people he meets with that he has discovered that by being still for one minute, he has increased his own effectiveness and that of the meetings he takes part in. At first a few folks thought this strange; however, they quickly saw the impact, and the idea spread quickly throughout both his personal and professional life.

Each of the above steps demonstrates commitment to prioritize the person and the time set aside to meet. It deepens our ability to access the inner wisdom that we spoke of earlier and access both our inner child and warrior. In these moments I ignite my curiosity and courage, which always enhances my ability to ask better questions, express empathy and really listen. When this occurs in-between, there is an acceleration of safe brave space, which unleashes individual and collective potential.

Holding open the safe brave spaces between two people is often tricky but highly satisfying when achieved. When two people experience safe brave spaces, it is like a beautiful dance with two partners who understand each other deeply and know when to lead and when to follow. It requires us to stretch both our styles and our responses. It is vital to understand when to share your truth and when to listen to your partner's truth.

In supporting the flow of this dance and sharing your truth, I have found it helpful to enter the conversation through the poet Rumi's "three gates." He suggests that prior to sharing your thoughts you should open three "question gates":

- Is it true (your thought or interpretation of your thought)?
- Is it necessary? (By sharing your thought, will it help or hinder, and is it helpful now?)

- Is it kind? (Will your comments build up or tear down? What can you say to help them hear?)

If you can answer "yes" to each question, then proceed.

Equally important in the dance is allowing space for the other person to share *their* truth. Two helpful techniques discovered during my years as an executive coach are "Three to Free" and "Two to One."

Three to Free is a memory cue, which reminds me to hold space for the other person to think about and share their perspective. As I have deepened my understanding of ME, I have become more aware of my instincts. Learning to trust and share my ideas has been an important part of my personal growth in becoming braver. As with any strength, especially something that is newly discovered, it is important to not overuse it and/or let it impede enabling safe brave spaces. Three to Free helps me to identify the most important insights to share.

Here is how it works. If, during a dialogue, something bubbles up as potentially important, I capture it immediately in a word or short phrase, so I won't forget. If later in the conversation, the same or a similar insight bubbles up, I mark a check or link to the original note. If it comes up a third time, I share it with the other person, usually by saying something like "During our conversation, something keeps bubbling up for me." I then share the thought and ask, "Does that resonate as true for you?" As well, at the end of the conversation, I review my notes and if something has come up more than once I decide, using the "Rumi filter," if it is important to share it.

The second technique, Two to One, supports this "holding open" of conversational space by reminding me to use my ears twice as much as my mouth. Many of us may have been told by our mothers that "God gave you two ears and one mouth for a reason," and after years of both coaching and being coached, I believe this to be true.

Two final insights to help you and your partner voice your truths and ideas more effectively are (1) to always begin with your "why" and (2) to leave space for their "why." Beginning with your "why" ensures the other person is clear about your intention. We tend to assume that others know why we are here and what we desire, yet this is often not the case. Leaving a space for dialogue is an effective way to engage others in your truth and provide you access to the truths of others. After sharing what is true for you, asking "What do you think?" or "How does that resonate with you?" are easy openings and access points to start a healthy dialogue. Equally important is *how* you share. Rumi's wisdom also helps us here: "Raise your words, not your voice," he counselled. "It is rain that grows flowers, not thunder."

Holding space for dialogue when you are sharing is just as important when listening to others share their truths. This is often more challenging, especially if their ideas and opinions are contrary to yours. Prior to sharing your perspective, it is important to show both your desire to understand and the fact that you value their input. When you experience the churn of disruption caused by a gap in perspective, consider it a signal for you to take on a learner's mindset. See everyone as a teacher, ignite your curiosity, and say "Tell me more" or ask "What experiences helped form your thinking?" This inquisitive approach sends signals of openness and collaboration which enrich the safe space for the other person and open you up to more meaningful dialogue.

Sometimes within these conversations we must bring forth an important and yet hard truth. This has been an area of development that I continue to work on, specifically being braver when dialogues veer into areas inconsistent with my core values. If you want to push deeper, try suggesting to the person you are talking with that you switch positions or sides and consider debating the issue from the other's perspective.

Reflect, Recharge, and Revise

The final step to improve the quality and consistency of the connection between YOU & ME is to prioritize and schedule time to Reflect, Recharge, and Revise how we Show Up with each other. Two techniques in this area that I have found helpful are (1) recovery agreements and (2) what a friend of mine calls "www... ebi."

An established recovery agreement simply acknowledges and

prepares us for the fact that, because we're human, there will likely be moments of negative disruption in between us. I have found that either having a process or a signal to interrupt the energy surge that begins to build prior to the disruption is a great way to minimize the impact on the relationship. I have often used the word "crunchy" to describe when I have reached a point where I feel my negative energy rising. Sharing that I am feeling "crunchy" about something is a safe way to express being uncomfortable with an idea or a point of view. Making a commitment to identifying shared code words such as "crunchy" establishes an early warning system that a particular topic may require extra empathy and curiosity. I have seen people working in teams use the "yellow card" (like the one used in football/soccer games) to call out issues or topics that may be difficult. But sometimes these stickier issues can't be resolved even with these early warning steps. In those cases, it is very helpful to have an agreed-upon recovery plan that sets out how you will handle such situations. This could include calling a time-out, seeking a trusted second opinion, or agreeing to disagree. One last approach to help create a pause toward recovery is to simply say "Ouch!" if you experience something that you disagree or are uncomfortable with. Agreeing ahead of time to using this word to immediately recognize these moments provides an easier entry point to "pause and explore," especially in moments of heightened energy and churn.

The second technique, "www... ebi," provides a safe way to deepen trust and grow together. At the end of each meeting simply ask, from the perspective of enabling a safe brave space between you and the other person, "what worked well... [it would be] even better if..." Doing so demonstrates a commitment to each other and to a learning environment.

With a shared commitment to working together through Knowing, Growing, Letting Go, and Showing Up, you will begin to create what the Gallup Q12 Engagement Survey described as a "best friend." When this survey was first published in the 1990s, many business leaders considered asking whether someone had a "best friend" at work rather odd and sometimes quickly dismissed the topic as fluff.

Many questioned how important it was to have a workplace "best friend" and how realistic it was to expect that to happen. I too was confused by this question until I had the opportunity to speak with one of the creators of the survey, who asked me what I thought were the attributes of my "best friend." Prompted by that question, I quickly described a best friend as someone who always had my back, who saw me for who I am, who had the courage to call out what I didn't see, who supports me even when they don't fully see the point themselves, and who is first to celebrate and acknowledge my successes. These kinds of relationships, which I had experienced in both my personal and professional lives, were ones in which I thrived and released potential beyond my expectations. The more of these "best friends" that I commit to cultivating, the more safe brave spaces I enable for myself and others. In the next chapter we will dive deeper into exploring how we might bring these insights to life within larger groups of people, including our organizations and communities.

Shifting how we more consistently Show Up between YOU & ME requires us to establish good processes and test out new practices. The following questions will help you collectively test out some tools and/or frameworks to lay the foundations that will enhance your ability to Show Up more fully in your relationships.

- What resonates most as "true" for you within this section? What most challenges and/or churns within you?
- Identify an area in which Showing Up (Starting Strong; Stretching Often; Reflecting, Recharging, and Revising) would be most valuable in advancing safe brave spaces in your one-to-one relationships.

- Select one exercise or tool to try. Share your intention with the person with whom you are in a relationship.

Reflect on and capture any insights you are learning from this exercise.

5. Safe Brave Spaces Flourishes through WE

From a place of personal growth and acceptance, we strengthen our individual safe and brave muscles. This heightened self-awareness and acceptance normally leads to the opportunity to accelerate potential through enabling safe brave spaces within our relationships. As we enable these spaces across multiple relationships, we begin to fully awaken the potential within families, friend circles, communities and organizations.

I have been blessed to live and work within these types of communities both personally and professionally. Most of the time they were led by individuals who were already unconsciously committed to the idea and importance of both safe and brave spaces. Each of these leaders had already embarked on the personal journey of discovery outlined in our discussion of "ME" and consistently modelled in their one-on-one relationships the critical components of "YOU & ME." Simply through a commitment to and striving to enable both safe and brave spaces, these leaders began transforming their environments, moving them toward greater potential and impact. In a few situations, those not in leadership roles were the spark that ignited the idea of safe brave spaces within cultures where this concept had previously not existed. Later in the book we will talk about how each of us has an opportunity to begin this journey no matter where and who we are.

As I reflected on those communities that have enjoyed success on the safe brave journey, I recognized some consistent attributes. Each of these organizations espoused or demonstrated:

- A clear and purposeful mission and vision bigger than and beyond themselves.
- A commitment to discovering, enabling and valuing individual uniqueness and contributions.
- A culture and supporting frameworks to release both individual and collective voices and contributions.
- A courageous community that respectfully challenged each other to refine great ideas and grow together.
- A "red thread" alignment to enable safe brave spaces through all areas, including strategy, structure, system/processes/policies, rewards/recognition, talent and culture.

When safe brave spaces are enabled within communities, powerful change happens. Each of us has the opportunity to choose to be a key ingredient in those changes. In order for safe brave spaces to flourish in a community, each of us must further flex our personal safe and brave muscles. The best communities to maximize your growth and contribution are ones that are aligned to your PCC and values work from the "ME" section of this book. Even if this doesn't yet exist, each of the following approaches can be impactful even in communities that are less aligned to these things. However, your potential for joy, peace and freedom is heightened when the alignment exists. This chapter will share some ideas and tools to help you to enable safe brave spaces to flourish within your communities.

Knowing WE

Just as with the other stages of this journey, the release of safe brave spaces within the community begins with understanding a unique contribution—in this case, the contribution of the organization and/or a collective of people. The habits of exploration and discovery that we have been building in exploring ME and YOU& ME enhance both the pace and the impact of our work on WE. As in previous stages of the journey, this work takes time and requires us to remain curious, courageous and open. Consistent with these previous stages, it also begins with Knowing. As you will recall, Knowing is about caringly and honestly exploring and understanding our current shape and state. Like your ME work, the effort to Know WE is about fleshing out collective values, purpose, vision, and culture through the lens of safe brave spaces. Once we have aligned to these critical components, a community can build its strategies and goals and bring them to life. Knowing begins with the investigation, capture, and declaration of three important components: (1) **values**—what we believe; (2) **purpose**—why we exist and the nature of our unique contribution; and (3) **vision**—where we are going.

These three ingredients are so substantial that we could spend hours on each. There are many books and tools found in the toolkit at www.safebravespaces.com that focus on each component. My hope in this section is to share some of the things that I have leveraged as well as some specific steps that each of us can take to ensure we are enhancing the ingredients that enable safe brave spaces to exist and continue to grow. Most books I have read suggest that you begin with purpose or vision, but my experience has always been that beginning with values is preferable, as they are the spark essential for creating both safe brave spaces and successful communities. In both my personal and professional experience, exploring values helps you understand the energy source and the delivery channel that support what you are trying to accomplish.

Values

The values of a community are the heartbeat that guides actions and decisions. They can change over time and although they are often influenced by a leader, they are more often a collection of the individual values of each member of the community. The core values are most clear during times of significant growth and/or challenge. As with your ME work, it is important to understand what you believe within communities, through the identification of what values already exist and which ones are required to enable safe brave spaces. There are many tools and processes that can help with the discovery of values such as the Real Deal and the Barrett system; however, I have found the most simple and effective method is to create opportunities for dialogue around what is important.

At Campbell's Canada, this step began in discussions with the company president around what we saw as the core values, especially in those moments where we observed bursts of positive energy, innovation and contribution. From these informal conversations, which continued for a few weeks, we captured on a flip chart a draft hypothesis list and a set of questions that we could use to investigate and validate our assumptions. With these questions we began our exploration in a manner consistent with our desire to engage the entire organization. Our approach involved simple dialogue sessions where we shared our intention of capturing the guiding beliefs and values that had made us successful, and asked two simple questions:

- What are the top five values and supporting behaviours that have made this organization successful and are critical to enable our future?
- What are the examples that you have seen that demonstrate these in action?

We conducted focus groups, which included speaking with retirees who regularly visited the head office/plant and who were honoured and celebrated twice a year (at the annual holiday party and the long-service award dinner). We accidently discovered that a couple of our positive intentions—to engage the entire community and to commit to creating safe brave spaces—sparked tremendous energy and momentum towards something special. As we held these connection points, both formal and informal, we were able to capture stories and activate our team members' hearts in ways that would be critical to our collective success and would eventually influence the global organization beyond Canada. We had the extra advantage that—at least in our head office/plant—many of the staff members were second- and third-generation Campbell's employees, which created further momentum and energy around creating a collective spirit beyond our organization's walls. Once we had collected input from across the company, with the support of a great external partner, we framed a core set of values, simple descriptors linked to both our heritage and our branding. This draft framework became the centrepiece of the second step of confirming our shared values and even more importantly making it "personal" for each team member at Campbell's.

Continuing our commitment to dialogue and creating a space where each person could share their ideas and concerns, we conducted discovery dialogues beginning with the senior leadership team and eventually reaching out to all team members throughout Canada. This discovery dialogue, which we will speak more about in the next chapter, incorporates safe brave spaces designed to allow someone with an idea to bring it forward and to get respectfully direct, uninhibited input to enrich an idea and/or plan. For these dialogues we followed a simple process:

1. Sharing our intentions and process to date;
2. Presenting the draft values, including the descriptors;
3. Describing what they meant to us personally (the president and myself) and where we had seen them "lived";
4. Asking and collecting participants' input around
   a. What resonates and where they had seen our values "lived";
   b. What didn't resonate and why; and
   c. What was missing, what might be changed, and what didn't fit—and why?

Taking the time to engage people earlier in the process helped accelerate both the openness and directness of the feedback. As many of the words captured in our draft values statements reflected the flavour of the input that we heard in the first connections, the changes that were required to the draft final framework were minimal. Integrating our organizational brand icons further added to the resonance and enabled everyone in the organization to easily identify and apply the values to their roles. The final version, which you can see on the next page, presented six powerful "C" words.

USED BY PERMISSION

The same approach proved to be equally effective in a Toronto not-for-profit of which I was a board member. This amazing charity, which supported refugee settlement, had grown from a small grassroots organization into one with a much larger footprint, including three houses and a significant advocacy role. As it grew, the founder, executive director and the board wanted to build on the core essence and foundational principles that had guided the organization's work for its first twenty years, while ensuring they equipped it to fulfill its expanded scope and range of impact. Following a similar pathway to Campbell's, and partnering with my former boss, Phil Donne, we began with a small group representing all areas of the organization, including volunteers, supporters, former residents, staff and board members, to review existing documents and discuss what we collectively felt were the core values and supporting behaviours that uniquely contributed to the charity. Besides identifying four values and supporting statements, we also shared what each of them meant personally to us and how we had seen them expressed in action within the charity. This dialogue was a powerful activity as listening to and understanding the unique perspectives of each person on the committee deepened and broadened the collective meaning for all of us. Once we had created this draft, we shared it as well as our personal reflections with a broader audience in the organization and asked this group to share their insights, input and personal reflections in order to help refine the original work. We also asked this group to share what resonated for them and where they had seen the organization's values and virtues in action, as well as what didn't resonate and what changes and/or additions they might suggest. As with the Campbell's situation, because we had engaged a diverse group of all stakeholders in the earlier process and focused on helping to "make it personal," we found that the changes to the original document were minimal; however, the additional stories played a powerful role in helping to activate both the connection to and application of the values in the context of each person's role.

Over the past few years, I have supported a number of organizations in evolving thinking and language around values to develop "culture codes" (see below for one example). The discovery dialogue process is the same as that described above; however, the output is richer and more specific, outlining the shared commitments of what

SAMPLE CULTURE CODE

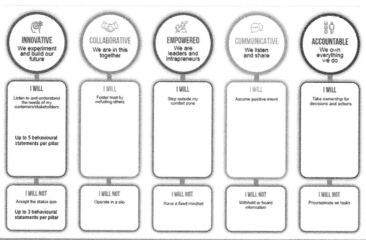

each member of the community "will do" and "won't do." These commitments to action, when integrated into organizations' people processes such as onboarding, performance enablement, and compensation, become powerful accelerators of both culture and performance.

Purpose and Vision

Early in the process of exploring values, especially in the stories that were gathered, we heard common themes identifying a shared purpose in the voices of team members. At Campbell's, the consistency and straightforwardness of what we heard from multiple generations of employees was astounding and provided us with the core ingredient to begin our exploration of why the company existed and what it wished to become. With this new insight, we added three additional questions to our community dialogue:

- What makes you proud to work here?
- What is unique about what we make/do?
- Why do you feel that way?

These questions helped accelerate our understanding around our purpose and identified a clear core idea—that Campbell's existed "to nourish people." This powerful insight was reinforced with the discovery of early writings by one of the company's founders, John Thompson Dorrance, who had stated that the intent behind the creation of condensed soup was "to provide greater access to nourishing meals for all Americans." This intention became a powerful link to releasing the potential of each Campbell's Canada team member, both individually and collectively, within ourselves and in the products we created for our customers.

In the work at Campbell's and in supporting others in uncovering their purpose, I have found it helpful to follow a simple four-step approach:

1. Conduct discovery dialogues (in person or virtually) to garner insights from across the community.

2. Review the input and capture common themes to help answer important questions such as *Who are our customers? What do we do/make/build? Why do we do it/make it/build it? What is unique?*
3. Craft draft purpose/mission statements guided by the following frame: *We're doing X (what), for Y (who), because Z (why).*
4. Refine and finalize the draft through good mission-filter questions—for instance, *Is it inspiring? Would it be met with enthusiasm or cynicism? Will it help you decide what to or not to do?*

Having established a clear purpose, we fleshed out how we might bring this purpose to life through a clear vision.

A vision provides a sightline to help realize the full potential of individuals and the collective community. For me, it's something that is both inspiring and achievable within the context of today and the yet-to-be discovered possibilities of the future. I add this qualifier because I believe that the best visions are like long journeys up a mountain; it is when you reach the peak that you discover that there is a greater, even more inspiring pathway ahead. At the peak you can see further, allowing a new expression of your vision.

This interpretation of vision is like the earlier interpretation of potential as "unlimited and constantly evolving," as you explore it through love, curiosity and courage. At Campbell's we began our process of uncovering our vision through our second discovery dialogue, starting with the senior team in a two-day offsite at a lodge in Algonquin Park. The location and design of the senior leadership session were both intentional and critical to creating an environment where each member of the team could bring their full self to the dialogue. In the next section we will talk more about the importance of proactively creating physical, emotional, and mental space, tools, and frameworks to enable both safe and brave to flourish.

Early in this book, I identified the importance of energy and love as core elements in releasing potential. Interestingly enough, the lodge we used for this important session, although exquisite and supported by amazing chefs, did not have electricity. That being said, to this day I have never experienced two days with more energy than the time

REAL PEOPLE

REAL FOOD

REAL FOCUS

Extraordinary, authentic nourishment for all.

USED BY PERMISSION

spent in this session. Grounded in the foundation of "ME" and "YOU & ME" work, and fueled by our now deep and shared understanding of our values and purpose, the location and design of the event captured and challenged the collective energy of the team, resulting in a powerful vision of "Extraordinary, authentic nourishment for all."

The power of this vision, and of others that have resonated with me, lies in its simplicity and depth. The statement applied both internally and externally. Internally, this vision was a genuine expression of safe and brave being released into a community, and became the heartbeat that echoed through the organization. The word "extraordinary" encouraged each person to be brave and to stretch themselves. "Authentic" reinforced the importance of believing and trusting in your unique contribution, which strengthened both safe and brave muscles. "Nourishment for all" underscored the commitment to growing and supporting both safe and brave spaces for everyone. This internal commitment led to an explosion of creativity and passion that resulted in innovation, efficiency and results. The external expression and commitment to "Extraordinary, authentic nourishment for all" of our customers, suppliers and consumers helped refresh and reconnect a brand that had been losing relevance and regain a sense of trust and excitement with all of those stakeholders.

At Campbell's and in supporting others uncover their vision. I have found it helpful to follow this simple four-step approach:

1. Ground yourself in the organization's purpose—why it exists and what it does best.
2. Expand your mindset to help envision the future. Two of my fa-

vourite exercises to enable this expansion are:

a. Visual Explorer—leveraging photographs to express and articulate the future state. Have each team member pick the picture that most captures the future state for them, and ask them to share why they picked it and what words best describe what they see. Combining the input into common themes provides a great foundation for the creation of your vision statement.

b. The Dream Wish—ask each participant to imagine waking up to find themselves in the organization's "perfect future." Ask them to capture and share what they are seeing, hearing, and feeling. Again, combining the input into common themes provides a great foundation for the creation of your vision statement.

3. Leverage the insights from the first two steps. Divide the participants into two or three smaller groups and have them craft draft vision statements guided by the following criteria. Great vision statements are normally short (one or two sentences), simple to understand, specific to your business, and future-focused. They provide direction, are specific and realizable, and challenge and inspire the organization to move beyond the status quo.

4. Review the drafts, then combine and refine them. Create a final draft, again taking note of the above criteria.

5. Engage the broader community following a similar process as described in the Values and Purpose section.

Knowing WE is so foundational to establishing SBS within a community that I'd highly recommend pausing here to reflect on who you are, where you are, what you uniquely contribute, and where you hope to go as a community. The following questions will help you begin the process and test out some tools and/or frameworks that are resonating most and are needed in this moment.

- What resonates most as "true" for you within this section? What most challenges and/or churns within you?
- On a scale of 1–10 (10 being "very well"), how would you rate your community with respect to creating and enabling safe brave spaces?
- On a scale of 1–10 (10 being "very well"), how would you rate your community with respect to (1) having clarity around and (2) living your values, purpose and vision?
- Which area would be most valuable to explore and expand upon further?
- Select one exercise to strengthen your selected area of focus.
- What insights are you learning from this exercise?

Pulling It All Together:
Creating Your "WE" Profile and SBS Plan

As with the ME and YOU & ME stages, as you complete the Knowing phase of Understanding WE you may find it helpful to create a simple summary for easy reference as you begin to share ideas within your broader community and with your partners. This double-sided, one-sheet document is similar to the "Being ME" and the "YOU & ME" profiles and is meant to capture your values, purpose and vision on one side of the sheet and your Safe Brave Plan on the other. It can become a valuable tool to guide the broader conversation and to help you reflect as you strengthen the safe brave space throughout our community. You can find the WE Profile template on the Safe Brave Spaces website.

growing

Growing WE

By ensuring that your community is clear and aligned in its guiding values, the supporting behaviours and your purpose and vision lay the foundation for establishing safe brave spaces within that community.

Growing, within the context of WE, involves implementing practices and frameworks to release the people, ideas, and actions that will enable your purpose and vision to fully come to life. Consistent with the work in both ME and YOU & ME, Growing WE requires a commitment to investing in actions and exercises that enable the safe brave space required to deliver your purpose and vision. These actions are designed to enable a culture which values individual uniqueness, releases individual and collective voices, and encourages a courageous community that respectfully challenges all its members to refine great ideas.

A foundational action that can be initiated by each person involved in the process is to ensure that as many voices are represented in these conversations as possible. With an awareness deepened through work on biases, privilege and blind spots, each person can ask and act upon three important questions:

1. Who's not here?
2. Why aren't they here?
3. What can I do to help change that?

If there is wider representation within the room, the follow-up questions should be:

1. Are we creating space for the diverse voices in the room?
2. What can I do to help ensure all voices are heard and considered?

I believe that no matter your level or role in an organization you can lead, influence and/or support these actions. Starting from our individual circle of control and influence, each of us has an opportunity to become a beacon for safe brave spaces. If you are a senior leader, you have a unique opportunity to model and champion programs and frameworks that will enhance these components more broadly and quickly. If you are an individual contributor, you can start any of the following activities within the communities of which you are a member. Three of the most impactful actions that I have found to grow safe brave spaces within broader communities are to (1) enable dialogue, (2) cultivate ME and YOU & ME journeys, and (3) create momentum.

Enable Dialogue

The foundation for growing safe brave spaces within a broader community accessible to all of us is dialogue. When each of us supports and enables healthy dialogue, it creates space for each person to fully Show Up and bring their entire self to a conversation. The existence of such a space is critical for bringing your organization's values, purpose, vision, strategies and culture to life. Throughout my life I have always been a champion of the idea of dialogue, and as I have come to better understand the importance of the concepts of both safe and brave, I have also realized that for dialogue to be most impactful, it needs to be intentional. It is through a commitment to healthy dialogue that safe brave spaces flourish in a community, and in order for that to happen, each member must bring their "ID"—*intentional dialogue.*

Bringing intentional dialogue to each interaction within a community brings to life what Priya Parker describes as "the art of gathering." In her book of the same title, Parker emphasizes the importance of being very clear about the purpose of your gatherings, the roles within them, and the expectation around them. These principles are equally important for the dialogues that occur within those gatherings. As the complexity of conversations and interactions increases in proportion to the number of people taking part, having a clear understanding around the intention of the dialogue reduces confusion and misunderstanding. Throughout this book we have been discussing the importance of energy and how to best manage and channel the surges that occur when those disruptions happen. A positive consequence of being more intentional with your dialogues is a reduction in the negative disruptions that can occur between people. Over my career I have witnessed both formal and informal frameworks to support healthy dialogues, and have discovered the following four key intentions that underlie most if not all dialogues within communities.

1. **Discovery dialogues** provide an open space for "input only" ideas to build upon a core idea, insight, or product. They're a feed-forward process to get "move ahead" ideas and input, which may or may not be used later on, and to spark innovative energy. These dialogues normally occur fairly early in the process and involve a broad and diverse group of people.

2. **Dissecting dialogues** (alternatively known as "holes to the whole") provide a safe space to challenge and refine ideas within an environment of respectful candor, with the intent of strengthening or evolving those ideas. These dialogues can occur anytime during a process and normally involve individuals who are connected to a particular idea or project (internal or external supplier, customer, partner, etc.).

3. **Decision dialogues** are intended to present and get a decision on an idea, project and/or action. These can occur any time during a process and normally involve decision-makers.

4. **Discernment dialogues** are meant to help participants see something more clearly. These are the "difficult conversations" where through an honest, respectfully direct dialogue within a community we provide a wider perspective around a situation. These require the fullest expression of both safe and brave as each participant must be equally curious and courageous as they bring their own insights and listen to those of others.

Through the filter of these four dialogue declarations anyone—especially the owner of a topic—can provide clarity of purpose, role and expectations. Whether you change the names or amend the definitions, a critical first step is to create common language and a simple framework to inform the intention of your dialogues. When we bring our ID and ask others to bring theirs, we provide permission to all present to bring their full selves to the dialogue, expanding the release of safe brave spaces and collective potential.

Besides naming the type of dialogue, communities that have consistently healthier dialogues also provide a framework to help guide those dialogues. I use the term "guide" rather than suggesting the implementation of a more formal process because we all know that any conversation is very fluid. As in a sandbox, you need to create a place and some rules to play while leaving lots of freedom to create. I have found the following six steps help to aid individuals in consistently activating intentional dialogues (ID):

1. **Prepare.** Before you schedule the dialogue, consider and be very clear about:
    a. The idea, process, or question that is the focus of the dialogue;
    b. The type of dialogue that would best support what you are trying to achieve;
    c. The participants that you will invite based upon the type of dialogue; and
    d. The expectations and roles of participants. (To allow all the participants to fully participate in the dialogue I often suggest also appointing a documentarian. As well, with tools such as Zoom you can, with permission, record the session.)
2. **Declare.** At the beginning of the session, declare:
    a. What type of dialogue this is (i.e., Discovery, Dissecting, Decision, Discernment); and
    b. Your hopes, expectations and roles for participants, including yourself.
3. **Share** your idea, process and/or question, including why it is important to you.
4. **Care** for all input, from all participants' perspectives. Enter each dialogue with a mindset of gratitude for their time, their unique perspectives and their willingness to courageously share their insights.
5. **Capture** what you hear without judgment and with a curious spirit.
6. **Close.** Thank participants for their contributions and outline next steps if any.

A commitment to enabling healthy dialogues is a critically important step to releasing potential and to modeling your commitment to safe brave spaces, yet it is often the missing component within communities. Historically, we have spent much of our time training people on feedback—both giving and receiving it, with an enhanced focus on things like candor and conflict. Although I appreciate much of this work, I wonder if it focuses us on the wrong things. Or maybe we are starting at the wrong point. I believe that if we begin with a commitment to safe brave spaces through the lens of enabling healthy intentional dialogues, it will speed reconciliation and allow for deeper collective wisdom and meaningful transformations.

Cultivate ME and YOU & ME

Intentional dialogue is also powerful in the previous two stages of the SBS journey: ME and YOU & ME. The more work we do in strengthening individuals and relationships, the richer the dialogues and the greater the collective advancement of the organization's values, purpose, strategies and culture. In my experience, leaders and organizations that make a commitment to investing in these first two stages build momentum for impact and results.

Cultivating ME programs requires a commitment, both in dollars and time, to deepen self-awareness around the values, skills and desired impact of each person in an organization. It stems from the belief that each person within a community brings a unique perspective and contribution, and the greatest opportunity a leader has is to connect these to the organization's purpose and vision. A simple filter that I have used to prioritize the investment in ME and YOU & ME programs makes use of two key questions. To justify investing in the program, it needs to deliver solutions to address at least one and preferably both of these questions:

1. Will this program advance team members in feeling safe and confident in who they are, what they bring, how they contribute and where they can impact?
2. Will this program contribute to advancing your team members' ability to be brave, expressing their questions, ideas and concerns while remaining open to those of others?

Prioritizing programs and policies by using these two filters will show a commitment to and belief in the importance of safe brave spaces. Some of the most effective programs and tools to help advance the cause of safe and brave within communities include:

Safe Muscle Builders
- Inspired leadership growth programs, such as those at Campbell's, leveraging exercises found in the ME section to help team members identify and create their Being ME profiles, which capture their individual values, gifts, strengths, purpose and plans.
- Internal coaching support, which is becoming more popular in many organizations, to grow this self-discovery process.
- Diversity and inclusion tools to deepen understanding of individual fears, biases and blind spots and to provide platforms for healthy dialogues.

Brave Muscle Builders
- Programs that help team members strengthen their voices, including membership in the Toastmasters International public speaking organization and workshops in improv, respectful conflict, etc.
- Space and support to help team members learn to trust their voices, such as innovation incubators, blue ocean sessions, hackathons, and so on.

These ME programs are important first steps, but are not enough in themselves. The most powerful shifts really take flight through how we approach and respond to others. Besides the tools and exercises shared in our earlier discussion of YOU & ME, each of us can impact others in our interactions by simply asking ourselves two questions:

1. What does this person need most in this moment to feel safer or to advance their brave?
2. What one thing can I do to enable the growth of either safe or brave in this moment?

By committing to begin each of your interactions with these two filter questions in mind and then responding with a "first to support" attitude, you will advance safe brave spaces and realize its potential. Being a first mover, empowered by a mindset of caring, curiosity and courage, is the second way to support the growth of safe brave spaces within communities.

Creating Momentum

The last action essential to gaining traction in the journey towards SBS within communities is to establish and support mechanisms to create momentum. Momentum is defined as "strength or force gained by motion or by a series of events." As with healthy dialogue, successfully creating momentum requires you to be intentional, planful and consistent. Each event needs to reinforce connection with and a positive movement towards your values, purpose, vision, supporting strategies and to your commitment to enabling safe brave spaces. It involves an activation of our full selves, including thinking, feeling and doing. It should be evident in what we see, how we feel, what we do, and what we celebrate.

Momentum towards something is really about building trust and creating confidence in a commitment, plan or initiative. An important first step is to reinforce belief in those things through various kinds of collateral, including visual representations of the commitments displayed on the walls, on the website, and throughout organizational documents. At Campbell's, a Vision Wall in the main hallway captured proof of movement towards our goals, as did a plastic card (the size of a debit card) that set out the vision on one side and values on the other. These tools, combined with the rebranding of all internal documents, represented important initial actions. We had to be careful, however, not to become one of those places hanging values statements on their walls that didn't reflect the truth of the organization and therefore quickly faded into the background.

What we see is important, however, because for momentum to gain traction it has to move from the head to the heart. For me, the best way to move from the head to the heart is by continuing to find ways to "make it personal." Many studies over the past decade have suggested that the second-most important reason employees stay at a company is "clarity of impact," while the first reason is a connection to purpose. These two data points reinforce the importance of the second component of creating momentum: capturing and sharing stories.

Earlier, we shared the importance of connecting each individual's personal experience to the values, purpose and vision of their organization. Having clarity around these important foundations combined with a strong bridge to what you do as an employee provides a springboard to enhance connection and engagement. Integrating "connection conversations" into existing meetings and gatherings is a simple way to deepen team members' ability to see themselves as part of the bigger plan. When we see the connection, we strengthen our ability to believe. When we believe, we increase our confidence, trust and acceptance of both ourselves and others. This heightened level of self-acceptance strengthens our personal sense of safe. From this place we are more confident to be brave with our ideas, our actions and our personal commitments. Stories shared also create further connection between each other. We discover shared experience, and we acknowledge others who contributed to the success. Like a flywheel, as we share momentum builds both towards the community goals and enhancing collective safe brave spaces. Sharing of stories provides evidence of what we are doing to achieve our goals.

One of the best examples of this at Campbell's, one that also provides a wonderful example of safe brave spaces flourishing in community, centred on the impact of a team member's commitment to bringing our vision of "Extraordinary, authentic nourishment for all" to life. One of our shared commitments as a community was to enhance the "nourishment" of our soups. Everyone in the organization had an opportunity to share their unique ideas and perspectives. Hilton, a team member in the blending area of our plant who was also a father and soccer coach, had challenged leadership and Research and Development to find alternate flavour mechanisms to enable us to reduce the amount of salt in our soups. His job was adding ingredients to the soups we produced, and he was certain that there were better options that could lead to healthier solutions. His provocation not only spurred a significant effort in this area, but we also chose him to star in an award-winning commercial that celebrated the delivery of a core strategy. Besides Hilton's becoming a local star, this recognition inspired others to bring their ideas forward and deepened everyone's connection to and belief in our purpose and vision.

Through healthy dialogue, cultivating ME and YOU & ME and creating momentum together, safe brave spaces begin to flourish. As communities nurture these types of environment, four additional steps will help support their growth:

- Tell the stories as you journey—both the great ones (what we did, who we did it with, and how we did it) and the not-so-great (what we did, what we learned).
- Make it visual by using physical spaces to reinforce and enable. Ideas include the aforementioned vision wall, naming meeting rooms for your values or key components of your vision, and establishing "idea incubators" throughout the building and on your intranet to provide avenues for innovation and celebration.
- Recognize and promote those who model and enable what you believe. Align your people programs with your commitment to safe brave spaces as well as your values, purpose and vision, including objective-setting, performance management, recognition, and compensation.
- Communicate, communicate, communicate … Celebrate, celebrate, celebrate success. Establish clear key performance indicators (KPIs) that track both the what and the how.

Growing safe brave spaces amongst WE advances as we nurture the environment through our behaviours and our processes. The following questions will help you collectively reflect on where you are and test out some tools and/or frameworks to begin these critical components.

- What resonates most as "true" for you in this section? What most challenges and/or churns within you?
- When considering the ideas of healthy intentional dialogues, cultivating ME and YOU & ME, and creating momentum, which area would be most helpful to focus on to advance safe brave spaces within your community?
- Select one exercise to strengthen your selected area of focus.
- Reflect on and capture any insights are you learning from this exercise.

Letting Go of What Hinders WE

At the beginning of the book, I shared that Letting Go is about forgiveness, forgetting and freeing us from the patterns and responses that inhibit us in creating safe brave spaces. As with each of us personally, every community is shaped by the values of the members, the situations that create experiences, and often the community's leaders. These and other influencers help shape an organization's culture, systems, processes and policies. These components all play important roles in releasing communities' full potential and impact. As we discovered with the ME work, it is equally critical to build in processes and frameworks to ensure you regularly review these components and, when necessary, let some go or alter them because of new insights and broader perspectives. In the section on "ME work" we explored the impact of the inner critic and in the YOU & ME section we discussed the you-critic. In both scenarios we uncovered the effects of these negative energy disruptions, which cause reactions resulting in personal mind storms and relational turmoil. Within a community, these same disruptions occur and are often amplified by the numerous stakeholders and voices found in larger groups. Sometimes these bursts come from internal collisions between teams, regions, or functions. Other times they are caused by external turbulence created by customers, suppliers and/or broader socioeconomic factors. The key is to recognize when they are happening and to establish mechanisms to manage and channel the energy surges. The good news is that the framework to help with this is similar to that used in our ME and YOU & ME work and includes:

1 Recognizing the common community conditions and triggers that hinder safe brave spaces;
2 Acknowledging and tracking your organizational energy bursts (both positive and negative); and
3 Implementing pathways to move from triggers to truths.

Although several conditions can cause organizations to lose focus on their vision and/or their commitment to enabling safe brave spaces, three that stand out for me as most common are *bold blindness, scarcity mindset* and *groupthink.*

The first condition, bold blindness, occurs when a community loses its capacity to see beyond its truth and reduces its willingness to be open and curious. This condition can have detrimental effects on both the safe and brave within communities. In bold blindness environments, we become less willing to listen to contrary voices and over-index on needing to hear our own voices and beliefs. Triggers that can result from bold blindness include arrogance and the tendency to dismiss ideas not widely held across the community or voiced by the loudest voices within the community. When we are "bold blind," we miss opportunities and often find ourselves traveling too far down the wrong path with limited options for recovery. Antidotes to this condition used at Google X and other technology organizations are "kill incentives" and "murder boards," intended to encourage team members to try and find holes in projects and ideas that might otherwise be missed as a result of "bold blindness."

The second condition, scarcity mindset, normally is born out of fear and can cause a significant reduction of the amount of "brave" within a community. The triggers that show up when an organization is suffering from a scarcity mindset are anxiety, worrying, and second-guessing. Scarcity limits creativity and creates massive organizational mind storms, which also blind the community to both opportunities and challenges.

The third condition, groupthink, can sometimes look like the first but normally is less about pride and more about taking the easiest path and falling blindly into a "we're all good here" mindset. Groupthink is defined as the desire for harmony or conformity in a group, resulting in an irrational or dysfunctional decision-making outcome. Cohesiveness in a group—or the desire for cohesiveness—may produce a tendency among members to agree at all costs. Triggers that often show up in relation to this condition are apathy and avoidance. Within groupthink scenarios, the community may feel a false sense of "safe" and experience what I call "brave atrophy," which results in low creativity and reduced performance.

Communities are complex, so these and other conditions will undoubtedly appear many times and often simultaneously. As with medical conditions, usually there are signs along the way that, if we saw them soon enough, would alert us to the impending issue. This happened to me personally a year or two ago when I was diagnosed with double pneumonia. Even though I am normally a healthy person who eats well and works out regularly, it was only in my recovery that I recognized that I had missed multiple indicators that warned me months before they rushed me to the hospital. This same scenario often rings true within organizations. We don't just end up overnight coming down with one of the three conditions described above; we have usually started to deteriorate months before and have allowed the illness or issue to grow to a point of serious concern. As in the ME and YOU & ME stages, the earliest indicators can be identified and mitigated if we conduct regular checkups and let go of anything that is hindering organizational health. A few practices that I have found most helpful in this regard are to monitor your organizational energy, understand your triggers, conduct regular SBS pulse checks, and leverage the opportunity to SAIL.

Throughout this book I have reinforced the importance of energy and learning to tap into early warning signs to anticipate and mitigate the eventual storms. For organizations as well as individuals and one-to-one relationships, this is best done through a reflective journaling exercise. An amended EEE for your team and/or organization allows you to quickly see the patterns that occur, more consistently predict the energy flare-ups, and identify ways to shift when they occur. Such matters will vary by team as they are driven by the collective energy of its members. Involving your team in both capturing and developing strategies around the following questions will go a long way in avoiding the more serious conditions described above.

1. When we connect as a team, what are the energy surges, both positive and negative, that we sense? Where and when do they normally show up?
2. What are the feelings that each of us experience when they happen (i.e., excitement, anger, annoyance, joy)?
3. What do they make each of us want to do? (How do we want to respond as a team, as a community?)
4. What can we learn from this and what might we change, shift or let go of to release the highest potential of our team?

With a clear understanding of our collective energy, it is helpful to occasionally conduct a safe brave space "pulse survey." The team can determine its frequency, and it is also impactful if included in a broader culture/engagement survey. Some communities have linked it to performance enablement plans, while others have integrated it into the closing exercises of a project team. It is most effective when it is kept simple and action-oriented using statements such as:

- Our organization/team creates a safe space that enables each team member to understand, accept, and trust themselves and others.
  - o The one thing that we need to do more of to advance safe spaces is...
  - o The one thing we could do less of and/or let go of to advance safe spaces is...
- Our organization/team creates a brave space that supports each team member in releasing the unencumbered freedom to stand for what they believe in and supporting others to do the same.
  - o The one thing that we need to do more of to advance brave spaces is...
  - o The one thing we could do less of and/or let go of to advance brave spaces is...

Conducting a team EEE and committing to reflection and revision based on that EEE through leveraging pulse survey input will strengthen the team and the community's safe and brave spaces. As with any journey, preparation such as this is important, and when freak storms still show up you just have to learn to SAIL through them. If you and your team members have been working through the ME and YOU & ME exercises, this will already be a well-known approach with familiar language. Establishing this as an agreed approach when anyone senses the team's energy and emotions building is a powerful way of collectively enabling a safe brave space by...

- S—Stopping and breathing > Request the team take a one-minute pause;
- A—Acknowledge and allow > Share your perspective of both the energy and emotion, request and be prepared to listen to the perspectives of those sharing;
- I—Investigate > Ask if what you are seeing/feeling resonates with

others. If it does, discuss what might be behind this and how this impacts the team and/or project;

- L—Learn and Let Go > Inquire if there is something the team can learn and apply; agree to the fact that the team needs to Let Go of trailing emotions and negative energy that might hinder progress ("use then lose").

An established process to enable the team to quickly pause, reflect and address energy and emotion spikes will help avoid ineffective spin and unresolved storms that hinder potential and reduce the likelihood of establishing safe brave spaces. One final insight around Letting Go is the importance of owning up to mistakes and asking forgiveness for inhibiting past behaviours, processes and/or decisions. Some of the most pivotal organizational transformations and recoveries have occurred when leaders and communities have been willing to be vulnerable through acknowledging and accepting accountability for mistakes. This is especially difficult when the energy bursts are extreme and have occurred because of the conditions described at the beginning of this chapter. Whether the crisis has been created internally or externally, those organizations and leaders who are committed to enabling safe brave spaces are consistently more successful in navigating the storm. Two organizations that modeled these behaviours are Maple Leaf Foods during the listeriosis crisis of 2008 and Loblaws/Joe Fresh during the tragic collapse of a manufacturing facility in Bangladesh in 2013. In both situations the leaders and the organization let go of corporate-speak and channelled the negative energy of horrific situations towards positive action by demonstrating both safe (confidence in their people and processes) and brave (quickly owning up to their responsibilities, apologizing and immediately declaring a commitment to action with a clear accountability plan). Through their actions, both organizations not only recovered more rapidly but also gained a higher level of trust and commitment from their employees, customers, suppliers and partners.

On the other end of the spectrum there are many examples of powerful organizations that no longer exist because of holding onto behaviours or processes that were misaligned to their values, purpose and vision or that hindered the release of safe brave spaces. One of the best-known examples is Blockbuster. Blockbuster was a once a fixture in every town and a go-to place to source entertainment. It was a destination for many families, and the coveted membership card gave us access to a movie paradise. In the late 1990s, Blockbuster seemed to be unstoppable in both growth and profitability. Fast forward ten years and they were announcing the closing of the vast majority of their locations. What happened to this powerful organization which had a clear view of who they were and a proven track record against a clear vision? I suspect that they had developed some or all of the conditions described at the beginning of this chapter, in the process hindering their development of safe brave spaces. Within the context of a safe brave environment and a commitment to regular reflection and Letting Go, I believe they might have more clearly seen the potential of Netflix and changed the trajectory of this once great brand.

Letting Go within community normally centres on collective energy and shared behaviours that are over- or under-used. Building skills to recognize when they occur and finding ways to release them quickly is critical. The following questions help you identify those barriers and test out some tools and/or frameworks to help you release the things that are hindering your community in this moment.

- What resonates most as "true" for you within this section? What most challenges and/or churns within you?
- When considering bold blindness, scarcity mindset and groupthink (or others that you might be observe), which condition most hinders the realization of safe brave spaces in your community?

- Select one exercise or tool to begin letting go of that hindrance.
- Reflect on and capture any insights are you learning from this exercise.

showing up

Showing Up Fully through WE

Showing Up is about preparing for and leveraging learning and awareness to enable safe brave spaces in every moment. Accomplishing this within a community is not simple. It is hard work because there are so many variables and influencers outside of your control. In any strategy facilitation session that I run, a key component is a regular review of the political, economic, socio-cultural and technological changes impacting the organization in question. This "PEST" analysis quickly unveils the complexity within which any community exists. The strength of your commitment to, and your evolution of, safe brave spaces within your community is bound to be tested and more often is a key factor in successfully navigating unscheduled disruption. Throughout this book we have described the impact of energy and the opportunity to recognize it, name it and channel it away from being a potentially negative, disruptive force to being a positive enabler of potential. As members of a community, developing our individual ME and YOU & ME capabilities will help prepare ourselves to be key contributors when unscheduled disruptors occur in our communities. Organizations can also establish collective practices to help ensure the community more consistently Shows Up and navigates these situations. As with YOU & ME, it requires us to start strong.

Start Strong

In our earlier discussion of ME and YOU & ME, we outlined some valuable frameworks to prepare for and enhance the likelihood of more quickly releasing potential through the creation of safe brave spaces. Building and supporting these kinds of practices is equally critical to ensure that we more consistently show up in community. Starting strong within community is all about entering with a safe brave mindset grounded in your values, purpose and vision. As we have shared, it is so easy to get distracted as you begin each day and each group interaction. With multiple interruptions and disruptions arriving from both within and outside of your community, it is essential that you establish straightforward frameworks and practices to help more effectively enter into healthy dialogue. Three of my favourite practices are (1) one minute of silence, (2) energy pulse check, and (3) red thread connects.

The practice of taking one minute of silence, something that I shared in the YOU & ME section, applies just as surely to group settings. Implementing a consistent practice of intentional breathing, reflection and silence, although sometimes awkward at first, can quickly shift energy and enhance focus for any team. The most effective approach that I have found is to do the following at the beginning of each meeting:

1. Begin by restating your intention, such as "We believe that our best work happens when we bring our entire self to a conversation and commit to being fully present. In our sometimes frantic world, we need to clear our minds and collectively commit to enabling safe brave spaces."
2. Ask everyone to put down their devices, sit still with a straight back, and close their eyes
3. Ask everyone to take three deep breaths. It sometimes helps to count to four while they are inhaling, ask them to hold their breath for four seconds, and then exhale to a count of eight.
4. Suggest to the group that if a thought comes into anyone's head, they simply say to themselves "Thinking" and let it go.
5. After one minute, ask the following re-entry question to ground each person in the commitment to safe brave spaces: "What is the one thing you will bring to this meeting to enable the release of our greatest collective potential through enabling safe brave spaces?"
6. Invite everyone to open their eyes and begin the meeting.

The second exercise, the energy pulse check, is a quick round-table where each person answers three questions prior to beginning a meeting:

1. On a scale of 1 to 10, 10 being fully present and connected, how are you entering this meeting?
2. What is one word that would describe where you are in this moment?
3. What is one thing that we could do to support you moving towards being more present, connected and fully tapping into both your safe and brave muscles?

Like the one-minute-of-silence exercise, this can be uncomfortable in the beginning; however, it really helps to deepen connection and awareness within a community. It is not about solving but more about understanding and supporting. Most of us are very skilled at hiding how we are really feeling, often saying "I'm good" when we really aren't. In these states we cannot contribute our best, and the contradictory and confusing messaging that we send to others and/or what others interpret from us hinders the creation of safe brave space and limits both individual and collective potential. Knowing where someone is at the moment, and having clarity on how you might support each other, is a powerful way to deepen intimacy, a key component in the trust equation that we outlined earlier.

The last approach is called "red thread connects." These take more work to set up and require a commitment throughout all levels of the organization. They are like mini muscle builders for enabling safe brave spaces and can be conducted on either a daily or weekly basis. A red thread is best defined as a constant underlying theme within your community. It is most often a combination of your values, purpose, vision and the strategies and goals necessary to enable their achievement. Red thread connects are structured 10- to 15-minute stand-up meetings with each team meant to celebrate achievements, provide awareness of challenges, and enable focus and alignment to effort and work. They begin with the senior leadership team, normally first thing in the morning. Once completed, each of those leaders facilitates a red thread connect with their direct reports, which is immediately followed by the direct reports holding red thread connects with *their* teams. This continues throughout the entire organization, so that most team members hear a connected and consistent theme customized to each level and function. A typical red thread connect might include:

1. Celebrations—Top three organizational wins and measures and acknowledgement of how this team contributed to the success, and specific team call-outs of other wins;

2. Challenges—Top three organizational challenges (these may be internal or external) and initial ideas to address them, followed by feed-forward ideas to help address those challenges, plus any team-specific issues about which it's important to be aware and gather ideas.

3. Focus and alignment to the current work—Prioritize teams' top three goals and capture what needs to be accomplished. Who leads what? Who supports what? And when are things required?

Stretch Often

Even before the Covid-19 crisis, in a world of VUCA (volatility, uncertainty, complexity, and ambiguity), communities have needed to remain both focused and fluid, often at the same time. This requires us alternative forms of structure, processes and decision-making. These new frameworks need to provide individuals and teams with the flexibility to shift when needed and also remain consistent with core agreements and guideposts. To enable this fluid and focused state, communities have discovered that they need to (1) define their "tight and loose"; (2) enable "deep work"; and (3) consider "cage matches."

Define Their "Tight and Loose"

Things that are tight are those that have limited flexibility and require consistency across the organization. Examples in this category are things such as regulatory requirements and adherence to values. It is best if this list is kept as short as possible; however, it will vary depending on the organization developing it. "Loose" things are those where the organization provides more freedom. They are often paired with frameworks to help guide team members, such as those outlined for healthy intention dialogues. Establishing clear "tight and loose" processes provides consistent and straightforward language to easily and quickly decide on and choose actionable next steps.

Enable Deep Work

Many organizations have recognized the importance in creating space for "deep work." Deep work is defined in Cal Newport's book of the same name as "the ability to focus without distraction on a cognitively demanding task. It's a skill that allows you to quickly master complicated information and produce better results in less time." Newport's research suggests that deep work will make you better at what you do and provide the sense of true fulfillment that comes from craftsmanship.

Prior to Covid-19, the idea of blocking off 45 to 60 minutes of time to focus on one thing seemed unrealistic in many of our over-scheduled lives. As the flurry of multiple Zoom calls comes under control and the realization of an extended work-from-home lifestyle has arrived for many people, numerous organizations have begun to investigate new and creative ways to support their team members. One of the things that seems to be bubbling up is the notion of slowing down and getting focused. This is not a new idea, as companies such as Google had previously implemented strategies such as their "20 percent time," meant to signal their commitment to allow team members to use a portion of their days to focus on creating. Although the consistency of application across their organization varies depending on who you speak to, there have been significant product and cultural advancements that have come out of this commitment. A declaration within a community of the importance of slowing down, getting focused, exploring and investing in yourself and/or an idea is, I believe, a key to releasing potential within a declared safe space. Supporting these commitments with physical and digital spaces to capture and share the ideas that result contributes not only to advancing those ideas but also to enhancing storytelling, relationships and trust.

Considering Cage Matches
"Those organizations with an authentic dissenter generate 48 percent more solutions."
—Charlan Nemeth

In her book *In Defence of Troublemakers* Charlan Nemeth describes the importance of healthy disruption and dissent. She provides many examples of and approaches to introducing diverse voices through the establishment of "devil's advocates" or "challenge network." In the Growing WE section we introduced the idea of scheduling "dissecting dialogues" as a way of enhancing healthy disruption within a safe brave space.

Recently I read about an organization that had introduced "cage matches" as a process to release healthy debate towards advancing an idea. I must admit this was something that at first that I did not think much of. I have never been very interested in, or supportive of, things like boxing or mixed martial arts (MMA), although I will admit to spending some time screaming at my childhood wrestling heroes and villains at the Brantford Civic Centre. Many friends have tried to convince me that MMA is about mutual respect and high skill that leverages a diversity of techniques. Although I am still not convinced by the argument in favour of these physical matches, I have come to appreciate something called "IDEAS Cage Matches." Sponsored by the organizers of the popular TED talks, the IDEAS Cage Match is described as a fun, dynamic, colourful event in which pairs of debaters ("fighters"), including current and past TED speakers, argue opposite sides of a question. They do so in a mock boxing ring with over-the-top smoke effects, lighting, and campy commentary. Though the format of the event is total pop culture, the content is substantial, thoughtful, and leaves the audience entertained, engaged, and thinking. You may not have the capability and capacity to create a full-scale event like this, but even a scaled-down version provides an innovative forum to help amplify the release of safe and especially brave spaces.

Reflect, Recharge, Revise

Just as in our work on ME and YOU & ME, the last component designed to increase Showing Up in community is to prioritize and schedule time to reflect, recharge, and revise your approach, strategies and plans. We can easily adapt all the tools described in the earlier stages to facilitate similar processes within a larger community. Key to designing these adaptations is to both "keep it personal" and "keep it connected."

Keeping it personal means ensuring that you provide the space and the tools for individual reflection around both the community's journey towards its vision and each person's contribution towards those goals. If you as a leader have invested in supporting the ME and YOU & ME work within your community, then this will happen naturally.

Keeping it connected first requires regular review and alignment to safe brave spaces and to values, purpose and vision. Equally important is to establish activities and tools to enable collective healthy intentional dialogues to reflect, recharge and, where required, revise the community plans. These can occur any time, including after meetings, at the end of each day, each week or each month, or more formally on a quarterly and/or annual basis. Integrating these meetings with individual performance enablement discussions can reinforce connectivity and impact links to the ultimate goal. Besides those previously mentioned in our discussion of ME and YOU & ME, other best practices that I have appreciated and implemented are (1) post-project "love and learn" sessions; (2) learning archives; and (3) the establishment of community corps.

Post-project love and learn sessions are mandatory closure gatherings following the conclusion of a project or activity. They normally involve only the core team but may be extended to anyone who had input on or benefited from the project. They simply require the team to debrief the project or activity around the following questions:

1. What did we most love about working on this project/activity? What contributed most to that outcome? What could we do to ensure this contribution occurrs in all future projects/activities?
2. What didn't go as well with this project/activity? What do we feel might have contributed to that challenge? What could we do differently in future projects/activities to help avoid a repetition of this challenge?

These sessions, which can range from ten to sixty minutes depending on the complexity of the project, are powerful opportunities to slow down and reflect, celebrate and learn in community while memories are fresh and before we leap to the next thing on our list of objectives. When organizations don't take the time to do this, they often make the same mistakes over and over, missing out on wonderful opportunities to experience and enable safe brave spaces in action.

The next element—establishing a learning archives within the organization—helps to ensure these qualitative learnings are captured in an easily accessible spot for quick retrieval and reference. Most communities that hold post-project debriefs focus on the quantitative data, and although this is important, it is often the qualitative data that has the greatest future-forward impact. The most effective digital archives are straightforward and capture the project/activity name, the project lead and team members, any searchable tags (i.e., client name, function, area of impact), and the love-and-learning insights and recommendations. This establishment of the learning archive combined with a requirement to search it before beginning any new project activity will save time and cost, create a network of sharing and supporting, and help avoid repeatable challenges while increasing the speed to deliver. Developing easy access via a learning archive app will ensure just-in-time access for all team members, further facilitating the plan.

The establishment of a community corps is another great way to deepen connection and gain insight into the external communities that you serve or support. As in the U.S. Peace Corps, a consistent framework is first established for connecting team members to those external communities. Over the past few decades, most organizations have recognized the value in identifying and partnering with a broader cause beyond themselves. The greatest impact is normally achieved when you focus your efforts on projects and with partners who are most aligned with your unique contribution or purpose. At Campbell's we focused on partnering with communities with a desire to alleviate hunger. This connected well with our products and our commitment to "Extraordinary, authentic nourishment for all" and resulted in a deeper impact within the communities we served. Supported by a commitment to paid volunteer days, Campbell's became a leading industry voice with food banks, not-for-profits supporting healthy eating, and World Health Organization food programs. Volunteer armies from all areas of the organization, inspired by this vision, took part in food drives, served in local food pantries and even created a highly nutritious, delicious, ready-to-eat product called Nourish, which was shipped to areas experiencing natural disaster and other crises. One additional benefit of a focused, aligned approach to the communities we served was to strengthen trust and deepen relationships with our customers (both the end-consumer and the grocery stores that sold our products) and our suppliers.

Earlier in the book, I discussed the impact of shifting to an abundance mindset. This impact was clearly seen in these commitments to social responsibility. As we modelled a commitment to helping to end hunger, others were inspired and joined us in this intention. This collective effort of an expanding group of supplier, customers, and team members resulted in record contributions to those in need and accelerated movement towards our vision. Identifying and partnering to solve a bigger community challenge in a way that is aligned to your organizational purpose and vision is a powerful way to activate the heads, hearts and bodies of your team members. Activating organizationally supported projects in tandem with suppliers and customers deepens relationships, creates connections, and builds trust between each other and towards your organization. As this trust builds, you enable safe brave spaces beyond your immediate community, something which unlocks and releases even greater collective potential.

In order to create momentum, I would highly recommend in addition to the three exercises described above that regular community reflection dialogues be established to create purposeful pauses to reflect, recharge and revise. Like those outlined in the ME discussion, they may include the following timelines and questions:

Monthly Reflection (3–4 minutes)

- What progress did we make last month towards our goals? What did we learn?
- Where are our key opportunities to advance our goals and to enable safe brave spaces in the upcoming month?

Quarterly Reflection (15–20 minutes)

- In the past three months, what new insights have we discovered through enabling safe brave spaces? What has been the impact against our broader KPIs?
- What are our key priorities for this coming quarter to enhance our vision through safe brave spaces?
- What do we need to do differently to achieve these priorities?

Annual Reflection (1 hour)

- Once a year take a deeper dive, reflecting on where you stand in relation to your priorities: From this reflection, consider:
  - How have we strengthened our safe and brave muscles?
  - How has our growth helped enhance our strategies?
  - Where do we want to be a year from now? What do we need to do or learn to get there?
  - What partners should we engage to support our plan?

In both the ME and YOU & ME discussions, we ended by sharing some key ROIs resulting from an investment in enabling safe brave spaces. Within community, the easiest and most impactful measures are *retention*, *engagement*, *performance*, and *referral* (team member, customers, community, investors). At Campbell's the renewed energy resulting from our work on values, purpose, vision, and behaviours that support what I now call safe brave spaces led to six years of growth in market share, revenue and profitability. Internally, it led to significant increases in engagement, including three years on the "Best Places to Work in Canada" list, best-in-class retention of talent, and an improvement in the individual health and wellness profiles of our team members. These kinds of results are echoed in many organizations that have made a commitment to enabling safe brave spaces, including companies such as Southwest Airlines, Whole Foods, Costco and Patagonia. Each of these organizations, who consistently outperform in the areas of innovation, engagement, profitability, market share, customer satisfaction, and effectiveness are described as "firms of endearment" in the book of the same name by Rajendra Sisodia, David Wolfe, and Jagdish N. Sheth. In addition to creating value for their shareholders, they also contribute on a much higher level to their local communities and the world.

These and other examples in both the profit and not-for-profit sectors model an exciting pathway forward that leaves me both encouraged and convicted. Over the past few years, as I have been gathering data and writing this book, I have had the opportunity to meet some inspiring individuals and communities that have made significant progress in their journeys towards the release of safe brave spaces. You can find some of those stories on the Safe Brave Spaces YouTube channel and on our Safe Brave Stories podcast, available on Spotify, iTunes, and Google.

Shifting how we more consistently Show Up amongst WE requires us to establish good processes and test out new practices. The following

questions can help you begin and to test out some tools and/or frameworks to lay the foundations that will enhance your ability to Show Up more fully as a community.

- What resonates most as "true" for you within this section? What most challenges and/or churns within you?
- Identify the area of Showing Up (Starting Strong, Stretching Often, Reflect, Recharge and Revise) that would be most valuable in advancing safe brave spaces in your community.
- Select one exercise or tool to try. Share your intention with the person(s) with whom you are in a relationship in your community.
- Reflect on and capture any insights you are learning from this exercise.

6. Begin Wherever You Are

At the beginning of this book, I shared the fact that many of us find ourselves trapped within a storm of rising stressors and pressures that are amplifying anxiety, fear and frustration. This situation has left many people with a sense of hopelessness, powerlessness and despair, resulting in record levels of mental health issues and costs in the modern world. The worldwide Covid-19 pandemic has exacerbated this situation, and within this context of heightened energy and anxiousness, we have also witnessed a positive eruption of brave voices around the world in response to the murder of multiple black and brown Americans culminating with the horrific video of the Minneapolis police officer suffocating George Floyd. If there was ever a time to choose to seek and enable safe brave spaces, it is today. But where do we begin? And how do we make it stick?

To answer the first question, we can follow the advice of C. S. Lewis, the British academic and theologian best known today as the author of the Narnia novels, who wrote, "You can't go back and change the beginning, but you can start where you are and change the ending." Arthur Ashe was even more direct when he encouraged an audience to "start where you are, use what you have, do what you can." Ashe lived his advice and, rising from very humble beginnings, won three Grand Slam tennis tournaments, was the first Black player selected to the U.S. Davis Cup team, and was the only Black man ever to win the singles title at Wimbledon, the U.S. Open, and the Australian Open. I believe that both Lewis and Ashe would have agreed that "It starts with ME." I have also come to realize that once you start discovering ME, you will quickly find yourself contributing to and enabling safe brave spaces for YOU & ME and WE.

Throughout the book I have provided many frameworks and tools to support your individual journey—so many, in fact, that beginning that journey may seem overwhelming at first glance. This last chapter is designed to provide a quick-start three-step plan, following Arthur Ashe's pathway by beginning by first *discovering where you are.*

Where You Are and What You Have

The great news is that *anywhere* is exactly the right place to start. It doesn't matter whether you are just starting out in life or near the end, in a position of power or an entry-level position. There is no one like you in this world. You bring a unique contribution to both creating and enabling safe brave spaces.

The importance of individual contributions became clearest to me during a period when I worked with a spiritual director. This is a wise individual who helps you realize and connect to your deeper purpose in the world. Normally this involves meditation, reflection, and practical application of insights. Six months into the program she shared with me her perspective that our world is like the most amazing new smart TV. When we see the screen, we are taken aback by the beauty, clarity and brilliance of the picture. The thing about a smart TV picture is that it is made up of millions of pixels and for its full beauty to be seen, each pixel must be fully alight. In the world, each of us corresponds to one of those pixels. If our light is either out or dull, it immediately distorts the best expression of the full picture. Every time we choose not to contribute our unique perspective, we lessen our world's overall brilliance and potential. The first step on our journey is to capture our current state of brightness, our personal level of feeling and being both safe and brave.

To help with this, if you haven't already done so earlier, begin by identifying your current level of Safe and Brave on the ME Map by walking through the following steps. (As a reminder, you can find this template at www.safebravespaces.com.)

1. Plot yourself on the safe brave map. How safe and brave are you feeling and being at this moment?

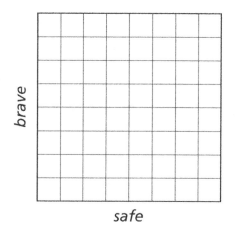

being brave
doing, actioning, releasing the unencumbered freedom to stand for what you believe in and supporting others to do the same

being safe
understanding, accepting, and trusting yourself and supporting others to do the same

2. Capture your thoughts around why you have chosen this location, first from a safe and then from a brave perspective.
3. Capture what you believe has enabled you to reach these levels.
4. Finally, capture what currently limits you from reaching a higher level.

Completing this quick exercise will give you a sense of your safe brave current state. Arthur Ashe's second step, "use what you have," encourages us to do a quick inventory of ME. If you chose to pause, reflect, and try some tools as you have read the book, or have completed similar ME Search prior to reading the book, you already will have done some deep work and possibly captured that work on your Being ME profile. If you haven't yet begun this more in-depth process, I would encourage you to complete this work first and at a minimum build a draft Being ME profile leveraging the template found at www.safebravespaces.com. Completing this process will give you the fullest foundational picture of what you bring and where you want to contribute. Alternatively, an interim step to at least begin the journey is to take a few minutes and capture your first thoughts around the following questions:

• What are the things I am naturally good at, things that just come easier to me than other people?

- What are my strengths, skills, and attributes that have helped me to be successful in my work and relationships?
- What are the strengths that others have recognized in me (i.e., family, friends, teachers, bosses, etc.)?

The answers to these questions will give you a good start in identifying some things you already have in order to "do what you can." You can also find additional questions and reference tools to help you reflect and capture your unique experiences and contribution within the self-directed learning pathway found on the SBS website.

Do What You Can for What is Most Needed Now

Once you have completed these initial exercises, the second step is to decide what you can do and what is most needed now. Doing so will help identify where you want to prioritize your focus in the near future. A simple exercise, the SBS self-assessment, allows us to do a quick pulse check on where we are within each phase of the safe brave spaces journey. With your deeper understanding of ME, YOU & ME, and WE, reflect and assess your level of understanding, acceptance and/or commitment within each stage (high/medium/low). As a reminder, safe brave space is not a "thing" or a destination, but a state of being and relating—not something you achieve, but *something you continually create*. As you activate it within yourself, you realize an ever-expanding level of potential. In my personal experience, this journey is very fluid depending on my environment and state of mind. Understanding that the levels of safe and brave within ourselves and in our relationships can go up and down, it is important to be hon-

	Knowing	Growing	Letting Go	Showing Up
ME				
YOU & ME				
WE				

est about our current state and recognize that even when we remain focused and committed in our journey, sometimes we lose focus and slip. The key is learning, Letting Go, and continuing our efforts to more consistently Show Up. Take time to do a quick pulse check now.

As you review your assessment, pick one area of focus for your ME work and a second area of focus for either your YOU & ME or WE work. It may be that you have more discovery to do within the area of Knowing, need to enhance your focus on Growing, or need to Let Go of something that is hindering you or a commitment to more consistently Showing Up. For each area of focus that you have identified, ask yourself (and capture your answer to) the following questions: *Why is this action important to me? What will it look like and feel like when I achieve this action?*

If you are having a hard time prioritizing where to start, I recommend that you consider an approach from one of my favourite books by Gary Keller and Jay Papasan, *The One Thing*. They suggest that the best way to focus your effort is to simply ask, "What's *the ONE thing* you can do such that by doing it everything else will be easier or unnecessary?" One of my biggest personal challenges is loading too many things onto my to-do list, which results in me becoming overloaded and stressed. Keller and Papasan's simple question helps me bubble up the most important action, especially when thinking about the day immediately ahead of me. One additional benefit it provides as I try to advance safe brave spaces across all three phases—ME, YOU & ME, and WE—is that it helps me identify actions that integrate across all three. As shared earlier, because these three phases are so interconnected, it is often easy to find red threads that enable the momentum within each phase.

Begin

Having identified your focus areas, grounded in a strong understanding of what success looks like for you and why, it is now time to begin. Two techniques that have helped me both get off to a strong start and create immediate momentum are (1) to envision your desired result, and (2) to identify your immediate next step.

The first technique is something that I have found extremely powerful in increasing both the clarity around and commitment towards my goals. It is a quick visioning exercise that allows me to settle my mind and tap into deeper wisdom and experience. It takes just a few minutes and requires four quick steps.

- Close your eyes and think about your current spaces where you have influence.
- Within those spaces think of one person whose space you can make safer and/or braver today. It may be yourself, or it may be someone at home or at work.
- Once you have that person in mind, think of one thing you can do to advance the safe brave space of that person. It might be something you've recently discovered or something you already know. Now visualize yourself doing it.
- Last step. Open your eyes and capture what you saw yourself doing.

The second technique is simply to look at the things you captured and then to identify and action your "immediate next step" that you can take at this moment to initiate your plan. By immediate next step I mean an actionable step such as call Bob, email Mary, text Ola, that you will take within the next short period of time. This simple choice and action are so powerful that they have consistently been the spark that has lit my path.

Make It Stick

With a focused plan in place and leveraging the techniques to get off to a strong start, you are better equipped for your safe brave spaces journey. As with annual new year's resolutions, however, we often start strong only to falter and fail as we encounter storms and disruption along the way. As this is an area I have often found challenging. I am regularly investigating new ways to help me "make my plans stick." Two books that provide excellent insights and tools are *The*

Power of Habits by Charles Duhigg and *Atomic Habits* by James Clear. These two books have informed and supported my ability to help to make my safe brave shifts stick. Duhigg's anatomy of a habit—Cue + Response => Reward—really resonated with me. He defines the three components as follows:

- **Cues** are combinations of stimuli (sight, smell, taste, touch, sound, thought).
- **Responses** are chains of thoughts and/or actions.
- **Rewards** are increases or decreases in pleasant or unpleasant sensations, emotions or thoughts.

Using these three components, Duhigg suggests that to build a habit we need to

1. Identify our desired result/response, focusing on one habit at a time;
2. Select a cue, a location, time, emotion or person that will trigger the response;
3. Design some "carrots"—rewards for reaching the desired goal— as well as ways to make them visual and support networks to encourage you;
4. Set up some yardsticks, touchstones and accountability partners to keep you on track; and
5. Practice the habit for at least 30 days.

James Clear builds upon Duhigg's work by proposing the following four laws for creating good habits. He recommends filtering our habits through these four laws to help to facilitate good behaviours and make bad ones more difficult. Although these laws apply to any situation, he provides an example involving healthy eating that will hopefully help deepen the insights.

1. **Make it obvious**. Don't hide your fruit in your fridge; put them on display front and centre.

2. **Make it attractive.** Start with the fruit you like the most, so you'll want to eat one when you see it.
3. **Make it easy.** Don't create needless friction by focusing on fruits that are hard to peel. For example, bananas and apples are easy to eat.
4. **Make it satisfying.** If you like the fruit you picked, you'll love eating it *and* feel healthier as a result!

You can apply these four laws to all kinds of good habits, like running, working on a side project, spending more time with family, and so on. Conversely, do the opposite for bad habits. Make them invisible, unattractive, difficult, and unsatisfying. For example, you could hide your cigarettes, add financial penalties, get rid of all the lighters in the house, and only allow yourself to smoke outside in the cold.

Three additional exercises from Clear's work that have been most impactful for me are the *two-minute rule, implementation intentions,* and *use of a habit tracker.*

The two-minute rule is a fixture of many best-practice writings around efficiency and effectiveness. It simply states that *if you can do something in two minutes, do it.* In order to create good habits to help changes stick, Clear encourages us to downscale our habits until actions can be completed in two minutes or less.

The second exercise, the implementation intention, is an easy-to-use way to formally put specificity around our intentions. For each action complete the following statement: **I WILL** [your desired behaviour] **AT** [a specific time or situation] **AT** [a specific place/location].

The last exercise, using a habit tracker, is simple: You keep a record of all the behaviors you want to establish or abandon and at the end of each day, you mark down where you succeeded. This record can be a piece of paper, a journal, a calendar, or a digital tool. Although I have many apps to track my fitness and meditation activities, to track my habits I use a monthly calendar hung in my closet. It's near where I get ready for bed, it's highly visible, and it helps me both celebrate my successes and hold me accountable to my commitments.

The Opportunity

As I complete this book, we are living amid multiple worldwide disruptions driven by the Covid-19 crisis and the heightened awareness and urgency to change systemic biases towards Black, Indigenous, and People of Color (BIPOC). Both situations are creating energy spikes within individuals, one-on-one relationships, and communities. Although often stressful, sometimes confusing and at times overwhelming, such challenges also provide us with an opportunity to choose a fresh path. The intention of this book is to provide ideas, examples and tools to support such a choice and—equally important—begin a further dialogue about enabling safe brave spaces.

With the recent demonstrations and protests around the world, the hope of change that I shared at the beginning of the book is growing within me. In contrast to the small number of negative reactions and actions, we are witnessing a surge of individuals and collective communities choosing to channel this energy to enable both safe and brave spaces for others. People of all ages, backgrounds and experience are choosing to stand together, beginning wherever they are, to enable healthy dialogues to release the potential not just themselves but of all peoples within and outside of their communities.

Among these shifts, wherever you are personally, you have a choice. One path leads to more mind storms, turmoil and scarcity, the other to peace, joy, love and potential. My hope is that you will choose to ELOPE, not running away but shifting towards something better. To return to an earlier analogy, we are all pixels in what has the potential to be the most wonderful picture of what we were intended to be.

Fred Rogers is someone who not only understood but lived safe brave spaces. He captured matters perfectly when he said, "As human beings, our job in life is to help people realize how rare and valuable each one of us really is, that each of us has something that no one else has—or ever will have—something inside unique to all time. It's our job to encourage each other to discover that uniqueness and to provide ways of developing its expression."

Imagine what kind of neighbourhoods and communities could exist if we simply lived out this beautiful call to action. At the beginning of his program, Mister Rogers always started by zooming in on the flashing yellow light, visually inspiring each of us to slow down and discover the truths within ourselves and about each other. Covid-19 for many people is a global flashing yellow light that is forcing us to rethink what is important and what we need to prioritize. Each of us has a wonderful opportunity within this moment of global pause to recharge our light, take our place to shine brightly, and to provide our unique contribution, enabling the fullest expression of safe brave spaces within ourselves, in our relationships, amongst our communities and eventually throughout the world.

About the Author

Greg Smith is an author, podcast host, executive coach and consultant with expertise in culture, leadership and performance. For over twenty-five years he has been known for helping to unlock and release potential through enabling safe brave spaces within individuals and teams and across organizations such as Marriott, Campbell's, and Porter Airlines. He is currently a partner with Lighthouse NINE Group and lives just outside Toronto, Canada.

Made in the USA
Monee, IL
30 April 2021

67324179R10105